COMBAT AIRCRAFT

160 Fw 190 *JABO* UNITS IN THE WEST

SERIES EDITOR TONY HOLMES

160 COMBAT AIRCRAFT

Malcolm V Lowe

Fw 190 *JABO* UNITS IN THE WEST

OSPREY PUBLISHING

OSPREY PUBLISHING
Bloomsbury Publishing Plc
Kemp House, Chawley Park, Cumnor Hill, Oxford, OX2 9PH, UK
Bloomsbury Publishing Ireland Limited,
29 Earlsfort Terrace, Dublin 2, D02 AY28, Ireland
Bloomsbury Publishing Inc.
1359 Broadway, 12th Floor, New York, NY 10018, USA
E-mail; info@ospreypublishing.com
www.ospreypublishing.com

OSPREY is a trademark of Osprey Publishing Ltd

First published in Great Britain in 2026

© Osprey Publishing Ltd, 2026

All rights reserved. No part of this publication may be: (i) reproduced or transmitted in any form or by any means, electronic or mechanical, including photocopying, recording, or any information storage or retrieval system, without prior permission in writing from the publishers; or (ii) used or reproduced in any way for the training, development, or operation of artificial intelligence (AI) technologies, including generative AI technologies. The rights holders expressly reserve this publication from the text and data mining exception as per Article 4(3) of the Digital Single Market Directive (EU) 2019 / 790.

A catalogue record for this book is available from the British Library.

ISBN: PB 9781472865069; eBook 9781472865052; ePDF 9781472865076; XML 9781472865045

26 27 28 29 30   10 9 8 7 6 5 4 3 2 1

Edited by Tony Holmes
Cover Artwork by Gareth Hector
Aircraft Profiles by Jim Laurier
Index by Alison Worthington
Typeset by Lumina Datamatics Ltd
Printed by Repro India Ltd

Osprey Publishing supports the Woodland Trust, the UK's leading woodland conservation charity.

To find out more about our authors and books visit **www.ospreypublishing.com**. Here you will find extracts, author interviews, details of forthcoming events and the option to sign up for our newsletter.

For product safety related questions contact productsafety@bloomsbury.com

Acknowledgements
The Author gratefully acknowledges the help and advice he received from historian friends and researchers, including Andrew Arthy, Eddie J Creek, Robert Forsyth, Chris Goss, Marc-André Haldimann, Histor Center AB Brustem, Tony Holmes, John Levesley, Jeff Litchfield, Hans Meier, Paul Moores, Georg Morrison, Roger Jean-Marie Mutte, Robin Powell, Andy Saunders, Hendrik Schoebrechts, Jim Smith, Andy Sweet, Peter Walter and Graham Young. Finally, a special mention for the late John Batchelor MBE, whose many years of research into the Luftwaffe and meetings with its former personnel were a part of the background for this book.

Front Cover
On 10 January 1943, several Fw 190A *Jabos* of I./SKG 10 operating from Caen-Carpiquet raided the small Devon port of Teignmouth. After dropping their bombs and raking the town and its civilians with cannon fire, the German pilots escaped across the Channel at low level and high speed. Fw 190A-3 Wk-Nr 467 'Blue 12' flown by Leutnant Leopold 'Poldi' Wenger was damaged during the raid, possibly from anti-aircraft fire or more likely by 20 mm cannon rounds fired by Plt Off Sam Blackwell in a No 266 Sqn Typhoon. Although the RAF pilot scored at least one hit on the fleeing *Jabo* before running out of ammunition, Wenger made good his escape and landed his damaged aircraft back at Caen-Carpiquet.
In this specially commissioned artwork, Gareth Hector has depicted Wenger's Fw 190A-3 'Blue 12' being chased by a No 266 Sqn Typhoon while fleeing southeast at wavetop height over the English Channel, with fires burning in Teignmouth following the attack by Wenger and his fellow pilots (*Cover Artwork by Gareth Hector*)

Previous Pages
Although it is usually associated with aerial combat against heavy bomber formations, the W.Gr.21 21 cm projectile was equally suitable for use against ground targets. A single launch tube could be mounted beneath each wing, as shown here on this development Fw 190A-4 at the Focke-Wulf Bremen factory. The W.Gr.21 was used against Allied shipping and ground targets in Normandy by several Fw 190 units operating as makeshift *Jabos* on and after D-Day (*Malcolm V Lowe Collection*)

CONTENTS

CHAPTER ONE
MULTI-ROLE CAPABILITY 6

CHAPTER TWO
***JABO* ON THE CHANNEL FRONT** 14

CHAPTER THREE
THE CAMPAIGN CONTINUES 33

CHAPTER FOUR
D-DAY AND AFTER 65

CHAPTER FIVE
DECLINE AND FALL 87

APPENDICES 93

COLOUR PLATES COMMENTARY 93
SELECTED SOURCES 95
INDEX 96

CHAPTER ONE

MULTI-ROLE CAPABILITY

The Focke-Wulf Fw 190 operated in the frontline with Germany's Luftwaffe for slightly less than four years, from the late summer of 1941 to the end of World War 2 in Europe on 8 May 1945. During that time, it gained considerable success and fame, and its celebrity status continues to this day. It was a worthy partner to the Luftwaffe's other excellent single-engined fighter, the Messerschmitt Bf 109. And, like the Bf 109, it grew from being purely a fighter into performing many other roles. One of the most important of these was that of fighter-bomber. In German, the term 'fighter-bomber' is translated as *Jagdbomber*, abbreviated simply to *Jabo*.

It was the Luftwaffe that was the first to employ fast, well-armed comparatively long-range fighter-bombers during World War 2, and the Fw 190 was at the forefront of this new but increasingly important type of warfare. A separate but closely related line of development led to the Fw 190 also being used as a *Schlachtflugzeug* (ground-attack aircraft) for shorter-range close support and battlefield interdiction operations.

Alongside the Bf 109 which preceded it, the Fw 190 became one of the Third Reich's principal production types for the Luftwaffe, and the aircraft served on all fronts during World War 2 where the Luftwaffe was active. The initial prototype/development airframe, the Fw 190 V1, first flew on 1 June 1939, its test pilot, Hans Sander, finding the aircraft to be excellent to fly. He duly became an important advocate of the Fw 190's development into performing a multitude of roles additional to that of pure fighter.

Several early Fw 190 airframes were employed in the development process to turn the type into a viable ground-attack and fighter-bomber platform. One of them was this fully armed example presumed to be an Fw 190A-1 or one of the numerous *Versuchs* (prototype/development) aircraft used in the whole Fw 190 programme (*Malcolm V Lowe Collection*)

Initially powered by the BMW 139 radial engine, all pre-production and production Fw 190s up to the Fw 190D series were fitted with the BMW 801 14-cylinder twin-row radial that proved to be a winning combination when mated to the type's clean, modern and well-designed airframe.

Ultimately, successful testing of the V1 and a plethora of subsequent development and pre-production Fw 190A-0 airframes resulted in series production of the aircraft commencing during the spring of 1941. The first model issued to operational units was the Fw 190A series, with the A-1 and A-2 production versions being comparatively austere models. Nevertheless, they illustrated the type's potential and were an immediate success on the Channel Front.

However, from the Fw 190A-3 onwards the true growth potential of the type began to be realised, and it was this version that saw the initial major development of the Focke-Wulf as a fighter-bomber. The standard A-3 was armed with two MG 17 7.92 mm machine guns in the upper forward fuselage, an MG 151/20 20 mm cannon in each wing root and (in many examples) two MG FF 20 mm cannon in the wing armament position just outboard of the main undercarriage attachment point.

Power came from the BMW 801D-2 radial nominally rated at some 1700 hp (although it was de-rated in service use when the usual 96/100 octane C3 fuel was not available). Distinctive cooling slots on the fuselage sides just behind the side exhaust ports were a major distinguishing feature of Fw 190s fitted with this version of the engine. So successful was the BMW 801D-2 that it became standard for several forthcoming versions of the Fw 190A series.

At least one A-3 was tested in the advanced French wind tunnel at Chalais-Meudon, with aerodynamicists examining the effects of fixing

Fitted with Focke-Wulf-designed carriers beneath its wings, development airframe Wk-Nr 636 displays the layout of the Fw 190G-3. This version of the *Jabo-Rei* pioneered the Focke-Wulf underwing fitments (officially called *Versuchs* Focke-Wulf Träger, V.Fw.Tr., 'Träger' meaning carrier) which could carry a 300-litre drop tank or a bomb. Early production G-series *Jabo-Rei* were delivered to the principal fighter-bomber unit in the West, I./SKG 10, during the summer of 1943, the type serving until the end of the war with a variety of *Gruppen*, albeit never in large numbers (*Malcolm V Lowe Collection*)

attachments and hanging stores under the Fw 190. This was a part of the development work carried out by Focke-Wulf that resulted in the creation of fighter-bomber models within A-series production. The modifications to achieve this came under the classification *Umrüst-Bausatz* (plural *Umrüst-Bausätze*), or factory-installed modification kits applied to standard production airframes as represented by a 'U' in the type's description.

Significantly for the fighter-bomber mission, the Fw 190A-3 was an important step in the creation of dedicated *Jabo* Fw 190 models, although it did not itself have a 'U' designation for *Jabo*-capable examples except for the U3 nameplate for a planned armoured version which eventually led through many more developments as the Fw 190F series of ground-attack aircraft.

A-3 examples used for *Jabo* missions would normally (although not always) have their outer wing cannon removed to save weight. These were the first real *Jabo* Fw 190s, but from the follow-on production version, the Fw 190A-4, the type was transformed into a formidable true fighter-bomber. This new version featured a number of changes, including a revised fin shape with a distinctive post-type radio aerial attachment for FuG 16-type radio equipment that replaced the FuG 7-type used previously. Prominent louvres replaced the simple cooling slots of the A-3 version.

The Fw 190A-4's armament remained similar to the A-3, although (as with the earlier models) the outboard wing MG FF cannons were sometimes omitted. In addition to *Umrüst-Bausatz* factory kits, a variety of field-modification sets had started to become available for the Fw 190 line by this time, usually concerned with armament additions for specific tasks. These were called 'R' or *Rüstsatz* (plural *Rüstsätze*). Armament options for the Fw 190A-4 included W.Gr.21 unguided 21 cm mortar rocket equipment for attacking heavy bomber formations and specific ground targets.

The standard fighter Fw 190A-4 version as a whole also introduced several important dedicated fighter-bomber conversion standards. These included the A-4/U3 with additional armour for ground-attack work and the U8 longer-range fighter-bomber. A lower fuselage centreline ETC 501 stores rack was usually fitted, sometimes in combination with other armament attachments. The basic ETC 501 was a universal mounting and could carry a fuel tank or a bomb, the usual load being a 250- or 500-kg bomb, or separately a 300-litre drop tank. The Fw 190A-4 was manufactured from June–July 1942 onwards, production finally being phased out in the summer of 1943, by which time some 900 examples of this important early production model had been built by several companies additional to Focke-Wulf.

By the time of the introduction of the Fw 190A-5, the aircraft was maturing into a potent, well-armed and versatile warplane that was

The normal armament carried by operational Fw 190A- and G-series *Jabos* was either a 250- or 500-kg bomb beneath the fuselage on an ETC 501 stores pylon. This 'Gustav' (believed to be an Fw 190G-3) is being loaded with a 250-kg bomb (*Malcolm V Lowe Collection*)

equally at home performing fighter, fighter-bomber, attack or reconnaissance missions. It was capable of holding its own against just about anything that the Allies had to offer, and the Fw 190 was well-liked by its pilots for its robustness, firepower and generally excellent handling qualities. Especially at low to medium levels, the fighter was proving to be a deadly opponent of the Royal Air Force (RAF) and the increasing number of US Army Air Forces (USAAF) aircraft that it was encountering on the frontline.

Production of the Fw 190A-5 was phased in during late 1942/early 1943, and lasted into the summer of 1943. A significant design change that was introduced on the standard fighter A-5 production layout was a slight length increase in the forward fuselage, which saw the engine moved forward by some 15 cm. This was to compensate for centre-of-gravity changes caused by the weight associated with the increased amount of equipment being fitted into the airframe that was adversely affecting the Fw 190's otherwise excellent handling.

There were a remarkable number of sub-variants and test aircraft that emanated from the A-5 production lines. These represented a significant effort by Focke-Wulf's designers to introduce more capabilities to the ever-growing effectiveness of the Fw 190, not just as a pure fighter but in other roles as well. The basic production aircraft retained similar armament to previous A-models, but a wider range of weapons and other equipment options were pioneered by A-5 batches or individual trials aircraft. As with the A-4, several A-5 models were important in the continuing development of the type as a *Jabo*. Significant amongst these was the A-5/U8.

Production of the A-6 – sequentially, the next A-series variant – commenced in the spring of 1943. This model was originally devised as a heavy fighter for the Eastern Front, and it introduced a considerable up-gunning of the Fw 190 line, with the addition of two MG 151/20 weapons in the outer wing armament position in place of the old MG FF cannon, which, in any case, were sometimes not installed or simply removed on earlier models. The fuselage and wing root weapons remained the same as for the A-5. To allow the fitting of the outer wing MG 151/20 cannon, the Fw 190's wing structure was altered and strengthened. Production of the A-6 model ended in late 1943/early 1944.

It was followed by the Fw 190A-7, which had originally been intended as a dedicated reconnaissance version and was built from November 1943 onwards. A major development with this model was the replacement of the generally unsatisfactory upper forward fuselage-mounted MG 17 machine guns of all previous A-series production aircraft with two much harder-hitting MG 131 13 mm machine guns. The A-7 and subsequent models featured a prominent bulged gun access panel ahead of the windscreen to accommodate these larger weapons. The wing armament was standardised on four MG 151/20, but in the A-7 a *Revi* 16B gunsight sighted the guns instead of the earlier *Revi* C/12 D.

The A-7 model was something of an interim version before the introduction of the major Fw 190A-8, which represented the high-water mark of the A-series. It was manufactured from February–March 1944, and its basic armament was similar to that of the A-7, but the lower fuselage fittings for the ETC 501 stores rack were moved forward 20 cm. Equipment for using the W.Gr.21 mortar rocket (hitherto mainly available as a *Rüstsatz*

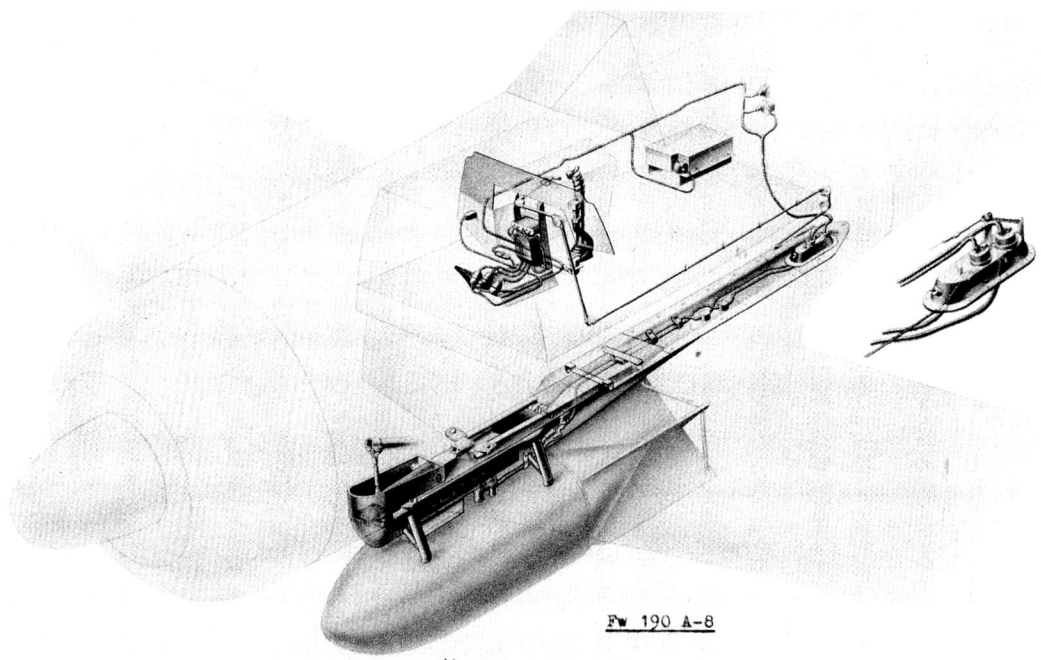

This drawing from a technical manual for the Fw 190A-8 reveals the workings of the ETC 501 stores pylon, seen here carrying an SC 250 250-kg bomb (*Andy Saunders Collection*)

add-on field installation) was built-in as standard. The prominent starboard wing pitot tube was moved on the A-8 to near the wingtip from its previous mid-wing leading-edge location. The type was built into early 1945, and it represented the height of Fw 190 production for the frontline. Indeed, it was the most numerous of all the Fw 190A series variants, with possibly more than 6500 examples being manufactured.

The last production model of the Fw 190A series was the A-9, examples of which were built from the late summer of 1944 through to early 1945. It was fitted with a new model of the BMW 801 engine in the form of the uprated BMW 801TS/TH, nominally rated at some 2000 hp. It featured a larger oil cooler and oil tank protected by a thick armoured ring ahead of the engine – previous engine models were also protected, but usually with thinner armour. The type's armament remained similar to the Fw 190A-8.

The exact number of A-series Fw 190s built is difficult to verify. A much publicised total of around 13,200+ is a decent estimate, but a lack of exact documentation, especially from the final months of the war, calls into question any exact figure. Similarly, some damaged examples were rebuilt or recycled and then finished as 'new' airframes to whatever current version was being manufactured at the time of repair or upgrading, thus confusing even further any possible final production total.

JABO DEVELOPMENTS

Additional to, and alongside manufacture of, Fw 190A series airframes, were the Fw 190F ground-attack type and the Fw 190G fighter-bomber. The potential of the Fw 190 for performing more than just fighter missions

Reborn as a nocturnal *Jabo* during 1943, the Fw 190 featured several refinements for night bombing. An Fw 190A-5/U2, which is believed to have been this aircraft, acted as a development airframe for the Fw 190G-2/N and G-3/N, with a strake above the cooling louvres to prevent the pilot being blinded by the exhausts and a port wing leading edge landing light/searchlight installation (*Malcolm V Lowe Collection*)

in air-to-air combat had been recognised from an early point during the creation of the type. Focke-Wulf's design team had built into the Fw 190's structure the strength and growth potential for it to be a versatile multi-role combat aircraft.

From early in the production of the Fw 190A series, the *Umrüst-Bausatz* conversion set U8 had been optimised to develop the aircraft into a capable and hard-hitting air-to-ground platform. The use of the Fw 190 in such operations gave the Luftwaffe the opportunity to upgrade its attack capabilities, which had been the preserve of such types as the Henschel Hs 123 biplane and Junkers Ju 87 Stuka during the early part of the war and, from 1940 onwards, the Bf 109.

The short-range ground-attack and battlefield support operations as flown by the Hs 123 became primarily the preserve of the *Schlacht* Fw 190F series, while the Fw 190G series longer-range fighter-bomber *Jabo* Focke-Wulfs largely superseded but never entirely replaced the Bf 109s configured for this mission profile. Additionally, later in the war, it was possible to find attack models of the Fw 190 that had been built using parts recycled from earlier fighter models of the type, in addition to those factory-manufactured with completely new components.

Because operational realities tended to muddy the waters between these two specific types, some frontline units flew a mixture of F- and G-models alongside standard fighter Fw 190A series aircraft configured for air-to-ground operations. This was particularly true later in the war, when the combat circumstances often resulted in some units assigned the air-to-ground role flying both *Schlacht* and *Jabo* missions with standard fighters reconfigured into *Jabos* using *Umrüst-Bausatz* conversion sets. Indeed, towards the end of the conflict, units tended to fly what was available to them, while the distinction between short-range ground-attack and the longer-range fighter-bomber became less rigid. In that sense, the *Schlacht* attack-configured Focke-Wulfs have often come to be referred to simply as *Jabo* aircraft in post-war parlance.

Also illustrative of the longer-range, fighter-bomber Fw 190G-series *Jabo-Rei*, this 500-kg bomb-carrying Fw 190A-5/U8 lookalike was probably photographed at Tarnewitz in early 1944. The unpainted oval-shaped area to the right of the national insignia beneath the starboard wing marked the location for a large 300-litre drop tank carried on a Ju 87-style fitment manufactured by Weserflug. This arrangement, which saw a single such tank carried beneath each wing, was used operationally by Fw 190 A-4/U8 and Fw 190G-1 *Jabos* (*Malcolm V Lowe Collection*)

Work to determine air-to-ground configurations and armament for specifically created Fw 190 *Jabo* production layouts had started with trials employing at least one of the original A-0 pre-production batch aircraft (Wk-Nr 0036) under the designation Fw 190A-0/U4. This may have commenced as early as May 1941, and had continued with other trials of early-production Fw 190s.

As eventually produced, the Fw 190G model existed virtually alongside similar developments with the *Schlacht* Fw 190F. However, the G-series was specifically for longer-range fighter-bomber missions compared to the F-series. This was known under the title of *Jagdbomber mit vergrößerter Reichweite*, or *Jabo-Rei* for short.

Development work continued with a small number of Fw 190A-1 airframes, which retained their standard machine guns/cannon armament but were tried out by Focke-Wulf with a variety of carriers for bombs and external 300-litre fuel tanks under the fuselage and wings. Successful development work, allied to testing at the weapons research centre at Tarnewitz, confirmed the feasibility of the aircraft fulfilling the longer-range fighter-bomber role, and a number of production Fw 190G *Jabo* versions were built, or created from the recycling of earlier airframes.

The early Fw 190G versions were directly linked to the fighter-bomber modifications of the standard fighter Fw 190A-4 and A-5 series, the Fw 190A-4/U8 later becoming the Fw 190G-1, while the Fw 190A-5/U8 grew into the Fw 190G-2. The combat range of these aircraft was considerably extended with the use of 300-litre external fuel tanks beneath the wings, carried on a possible variety of stores racks. Initially, streamlined Ju 87-type Weserflug-manufactured mountings were used, which unsatisfactorily reduced top speed. Fully laden with a 300-litre drop tank beneath each wing on the Weserflug mountings, and with a 500-kg bomb on the centreline ETC 501 pylon, the Fw 190G-1's top speed fell alarmingly to less than 300 mph. Both Messerschmitt and Focke-Wulf addressed this problem with their own far less cumbersome, simplified pylons. The Messerschmitt unit appears to have been used principally on Fw 190G-2 *Jabos*, while the in-house

Amongst the largest ordnance ever used operationally by Fw 190 *Jabos* was the 1000-kg bomb, seen here in SC 1000 form under trials, probably at Tarnewitz. Units such as *Sonderstaffel Einhorn* and elements of the secretive KG 200 appear to have employed this munition, the former operationally against the Nijmegen bridges during September 1944 (*EN Archive*)

Focke-Wulf structure was most commonly fitted to the Fw 190G-3.

Usually (but not always), these fighter-bombers dispensed with the fuselage-mounted machine guns as well as the outer wing cannon, limiting the internal armament to wing root-mounted MG 151/20 cannon. In this configuration, and with a 500-kg bomb on the centreline underfuselage ETC 501 bomb rack and a 300-litre fuel tank beneath each wing, a range of up to approximately 925 miles could be achieved. Just when the A-4/U8 and A-5/U8 were re-designated as the G-1 and G-2 respectively has become muddied by a number of *Reichsluftfahrtministerium* (German Air Ministry – RLM) documents giving different dates for this changeover – certainly sometime in mid-1943 appears possible.

They were followed by the Fw 190G-3 model, which was the first of the G-series that did not have a direct link to the original Fw 190A *Jabo* conversions of the standard fighter A-4 and A-5, although it did include some features tried out on the A-5/U13 modification standard. In layout, the aircraft was based on the A-6 configuration, but it was a stand-alone production version, with manufacture commencing during the summer of 1943. This model included a PKS 12 autopilot and, like the G-2 version, was available for night operations with flame dampers on the visible fuselage side exhausts.

The planned G-4 to G-7 models did not attain manufacturing status, leaving the Fw 190G-8 as the last of the G-series production aircraft. Based on the layout and equipment of the Fw 190A-8, the G-8 nevertheless usually only carried wing root MG 151/20 cannon without the A-8's fuselage-mounted MG 131 machine-guns (although the bulged gun access panel for these was retained on most airframes). Underwing stores including 50-kg bombs or 300-litre drop tanks could be carried on ETC 50, ETC 71 or ETC 503 racks. With a 500-kg bomb beneath the fuselage and a 300-litre external fuel tank beneath each wing, the G-8 had an impressive potential range of some 1045 miles at an average speed of approximately 265 mph.

Production began in the late summer of 1943 and continued until approximately March 1944, by which time at least 146 examples had been built, although this figure is probably nearer to 800. Manufacturing of the aircraft was abandoned in the spring of 1944 so that all efforts could be put into production of the Fw 190F-8, the need for the G-series long-range fighter-bomber having become reduced due to the increasingly unfavourable military situation. Several possible manufacturing totals have been suggested for overall Fw 190G production, with approximately 1300 nowadays being most favoured. However, in reality, any figure is only a rough estimate due to missing documentation and the recycling of older airframes, including the construction of individual aircraft from damaged machines.

CHAPTER TWO

JABO ON THE CHANNEL FRON

Following the defeat of France in June 1940, the Germans built up a formidable array of fighter and bomber assets on French airfields in preparation for the planned aerial assault against the British Isles. But the Luftwaffe's lack of overall success in the subsequent Battle of Britain from July 1940 onwards, and the completely separate intended invasion of the Soviet Union in June 1941, had subsequently denuded this large number of operational units and their assets. By mid-1941 only two *Jagdgeschwader* (JG), JGs 2 and 26, remained on what had come to be called the 'Channel Front' facing Britain, both of these units being equipped with the Bf 109. Originally flying the Bf 109E, by mid-1941 the improved and more powerful Bf 109F was coming into widespread service with both units.

One type of warplane that had proven to be of military value during the Battle of Britain was the fighter-bomber, which the Luftwaffe had successfully pioneered as a stand-alone combatant during the summer of 1940. The use of fighter aircraft as makeshift air-to-ground platforms had already worked successfully for Germany's *Legion Condor* in the Spanish Civil War, which ended on 1 April 1939. And in a somewhat ad hoc fashion, Bf 109s had been used similarly during the attack on Poland commencing on 1 September 1939, and in the subsequent *Blitzkrieg* period that culminated in the defeat of France.

In the early days of the Battle of Britain, the rise of the fighter-bomber took on a much more organised and well-executed form with the

One of the earliest Focke-Wulf fighter-bombers in France was 'Black 6' of 10./JG 26, seen here with its engine running at Saint-Omer-Wizernes. The original *Jabo* Fw 190A-2, A-3 and A-4/U8 airframes were similar when seen from some angles, thus making them difficult to tell apart, especially if the vertical tail could not be seen. The stylised bomb motif (a modified 'bar' from the 'chevron and bar' marking displayed by all *Jabo* units on the Channel Front) can just be seen at the extreme left of the photograph. It was quite different to the bomb symbol that had adorned the *Staffel*'s Bf 109F *Jabos*, which had been replaced by the Focke-Wulfs during the summer of 1942 *(Malcolm V Lowe Collection)* establishment of *Erprobungsgruppe* (ErprGr) 210 on 1 July 1940 at Köln-Ostheim. Its 3. *Staffel* was equipped with *Jabo* Bf 109E fighters that were specifically configured to carry a bomb beneath the fuselage. The unit's pilots were specially trained in air-to-ground tactics, and as such, were the first of a new breed of aviators.

Led by Oberleutnant Otto Hintze, 3./ErprGr 210 moved to the French airfield of Denain-Prouvy near Valenciennes on 10 July (the official start of the Battle of Britain according to the British Air Ministry), from where it commenced launching fighter-bomber operations. During the third week of July the unit began taking a toll of maritime targets.

Having thus pioneered *Jabo* operations, soon 3./ErprGr 210 was joined by other units dedicated to mounting fighter-bomber missions over England. The second organisation thus committed was *Lehrgeschwader* (LG) 2. In Luftwaffe parlance, *Lehrgeschwader* has an ambiguous meaning that has been described as an operational training or demonstration unit. However, the two principal *Lehrgeschwader* that existed during the war, LGs 1 and 2, both took on fully operational frontline roles and saw a considerable amount of combat.

Within LG 2, II.(*Schlacht*)/LG 2 was the *Geschwader*'s attack component, and it was also destined to play a key role in the use of the *Jabo* Bf 109E during 1940. The operational debut for LG 2's Bf 109E *Jabo* force came on 2 September 1940. Now declared fully operational within *Luftflotte* 2, II.(S)/LG 2 undertook its first sorties during a day of raids by the Luftwaffe against various targets in Kent and the Thames Estuary.

As the Battle of Britain progressed, the success of the specific fighter-bomber missions flown by 3./ErprGr 210 and II.(S)/LG 2 proved beyond doubt the validity of the concept. In one of his characteristically bombastic pronouncements, the leader of the Luftwaffe, Reichsmarschall Hermann Göring, decreed that each *Jagdgeschwader* had to form or convert several *Staffeln* to fly dedicated fighter-bomber operations. It was on 2 September that this now infamous announcement was made by Göring regarding the need for each *Jagdgeschwader* to convert three of its *Staffeln* into specialist *Jabo* units. When news of this major alteration to the pursuit of the air war reached the frontline units, there was a very mixed reaction.

Subsequently, some *Jagdgeschwader* were reluctant to carry out this plan, while others were less reticent. Several officers in higher authority were unhappy. The veteran fighter pilot Generalmajor Theodor Osterkamp, who had led Bf 109E-equipped JG 51 during the *Blitzkrieg* period and into the early stages of the Battle of Britain, had been moved from his role as the unit's *Geschwaderkommodore* to become the *Jagdfliegerführer* 1 of the fighter units in *Luftflotte* 2 during the latter part of the campaign. He was unenthusiastic about the decision to make fighter pilots deliver bombs;

'The order for each *Geschwader* to form its own *Jabo Staffeln* came from the highest level. We were left to sort it out ourselves. There was great concern amongst many of us that this was going to be difficult to achieve, and it would distract from our main purpose.'

Osterkamp was also apprehensive about the morale of his pilots;

'I could already see that some of my fighter leaders, and their over-worked airmen, were unhappy with these changes.'

Significantly for events later in the war, two of the *Geschwader* that did eventually carry through the principle of forming *Jabo* units within their ranks were JG 2 'Richthofen' and JG 26 'Schlageter'. For the latter, 3., 4. and 9. *Staffeln* were converted into fighter-bomber squadrons. JG 26's *Jabos* subsequently featured in the final stages of the Battle of Britain, and beyond.

Within JG 2, 2., 6. and 7. *Staffeln* became *Jabo* units, but these were not involved in the Battle of Britain or its immediate aftermath. Indeed, it was not until November that pilots of 2./JG 2 were initially posted to Denain to work with 3./ErprGr 210 and LG 2 on converting into the fighter-bomber role, only becoming operational several months later.

The Battle of Britain officially concluded on 31 October 1940. The Germans had failed to achieve the aim of defeating the RAF, thus clearing the way for a cross-Channel invasion during the summer and autumn of 1940. In the early months of 1941 the emphasis of German strategy was irrevocably turning towards the Soviet Union. This contributed to a gradual run-down of Luftwaffe units facing Britain that continued well into 1941, with more and more *Gruppen* withdrawn back to Germany or to further-flung occupied parts of the Continent.

Indeed, during that time only JGs 2 and 26 remained to face the RAF on the Channel Front. But they were formidable adversaries, and in addition to their subsequent considerable fighter activity, both played a central role in the use of *Jabos* against British targets in the coming three years. These two units became specifically involved in fighter-bomber operations during 1941 against targets in southern England and in the English Channel, eventually using the new Bf 109F. Significantly, both were later to play a key role in Fw 190 *Jabo* operations against England.

JGs 2 and 26 rapidly became established as daunting opponents for the RAF aircraft that were increasingly venturing across the English Channel to draw the Luftwaffe to battle and to attack specific targets in the months following the cessation of the Battle of Britain. They were also basically alone in providing fighter cover over the Channel Front due to the many other fighter *Geschwader* formerly based there being readied for the coming onslaught against the Soviet Union and, therefore, gradually but increasingly being removed from the West.

During the early months of 1941, JG 2's *Stab*, I. and II. *Gruppen* had been based at Beaumont-le-Roger, with III. *Gruppe* at Bernay, all within *Luftflotte* 3. JG 26, however, had been located further east at Abbeville-Drucat as a part of *Luftflotte* 2. Of these bases, the former *Armée de l'Air* airfield of Beaumont-le-Roger was well situated, being roughly equidistant between the Pas-de-Calais and the Cherbourg peninsula, and therefore within striking distance of a large swathe of southern England. Similarly, Abbeville and airfields in the Pas-de-Calais were suitably located for action over southeast England and London.

Within JG 2, its three *Staffeln* specifically delegated to *Jabo* operations – 2., 6. and 7. *Staffeln* – were each drawn from a different *Gruppe*. A fighter *Geschwader* at that time was comprised of three *Gruppen*, each with three *Staffeln*, although this changed later in the war. Leading 7./JG 2 was the accomplished fighter pilot Oberleutnant Werner Machold. 2. *Staffel* was headed by Oberleutnant Siegfried Bethke, with Oberleutnant

The leading light of 10./JG 2's *Jabo* effort was Oberleutnant (later Hauptmann) Frank Liesendahl, the successful *Staffelkapitän* of 13./JG 2. A veteran of combat in Poland (with II./ZG 1), the *Blitzkrieg* in France and the Battle of Britain, he had helped perfect the tactics – including the 'Liesendahl Method' – that were employed so effectively by *Jabo* Bf 109F fighter-bombers on the Channel Front during 1941–42. Having undertaken many missions in the Bf 109F, Liesendahl's association with the Fw 190A *Jabo* was to be a brief one. He was shot down and killed attacking a tanker and its escorts off Berry Head on 17 July 1942 (*Chris Goss Collection*)

(later Hauptmann) Frank Liesendahl in charge of 6./JG 2. The latter, in particular, was instrumental in developing Luftwaffe fighter-bomber tactics, and he was to later play an important, if brief, part in the integration of the Fw 190 into *Jabo* operations over the Channel Front.

In service, the *Jabo* Bf 109Fs proved ideal for continuing and extending the work already carried out by the Bf 109E fighter-bombers during the Battle of Britain and subsequent months. The fight still needed to be taken to the British on the Channel Front, and the new F-series was the ideal type with which to continue these operations in the summer and autumn of 1941. And so began a new phase of organised *Jabo* attacks against targets in southern England, sometimes referred to as 'tip and run' sorties, although they are much more widely known as 'hit and run' raids.

A significant amount of work was carried out by 6./JG 2's Oberleutnant Frank Liesendahl to develop and perfect *Jabo* operations. The type of fighter-bomber attack that he worked on became colloquially known as the Liesendahl Verfahren ('Liesendahl Method'). It involved a very fast initial low-level approach at virtually wave-top or tree-top height at a speed of around 280 mph. At just over a mile from the intended target, the pilot would effect a rapid climb to an altitude of 1650 ft before levelling off. A dive towards the target was then made at a preferred angle of three degrees with air speed increasing to around 340 mph. Using the aircraft's *Revi* gunsight, the pilot would then pull up and release the 250-kg bomb beneath the fuselage. By so doing, he effectively lobbed the weapon towards the target. With considerable practice, this method of attack could be made very accurate and highly effective.

The commander of JG 2, Major Walter Oesau, was encouraged by Liesendahl to create a squadron within the *Geschwader* specifically for fighter-bomber operations. On 10 November 1941, a new, dedicated *Jabo Staffel*, 13./JG 2, was established at Beaumont-le-Roger. At the time, it was unusual for fighter *Geschwader* to have an operational 13. *Staffel*, and for paperwork purposes the new unit was delegated to II./JG 2. In practice, however, 13./JG 2 acted largely independently under Liesendahl's leadership.

To begin with, the unit embarked on a long training period in which Liesendahl's fighter-bomber theories were defined and training was undertaken. Some of the pilots who had flown in JG 2's previous *Jabo Staffeln* joined the new unit. The *Staffel* officially became operational on 18 February 1942, equipped with fighter-bomber Bf 109Fs. It began mounting sorties as soon as the weather improved, having been given responsibility for attacking targets in the western Channel area of southwest England. Up to that point, there had been a lull in significant fighter-bomber activity over southern England for several months, but the coming into service of 13./JG 2 rapidly changed that situation.

For the time being, Liesendahl's *Jabos* were able to wreak havoc on the coastal towns of Devon. Small local convoys and harbour installations became a familiar set of targets, with Torquay and Brixham being particularly hard hit.

At the start of April 1942, 13./JG 2 was re-designated 10./JG 2 (or, to give the *Staffel* its full title, 10.(*Jabo*)/JG 2). That month saw a considerable expansion in *Jabo* attacks. Missions often included just a four-aircraft *Schwarm*, marking them out as totally different to the large-scale *Jabo* attacks of the later Battle of Britain period. JG 2's pilots came to know the western Channel well, with Devon's prominent landmarks and the distinctive shape of its coastline making the job of finding specific targets an easy one as the aircraft headed northwest at low-level.

JG 26 'Schlageter', then under the command of Major Gerhard Schöpfel, was ordered to form its own dedicated *Jabo Staffel* on 10 March 1942 at Saint-Omer-Arques along the same lines as 13./JG 2. This new *Staffel* was designated 10./JG 26 (officially 10.(*Jabo*)/JG 26) and commanded by Hauptmann Karl Plunser. It began operations during April 1942, tasked with covering the southeast of England.

During the following weeks, the two *Jabo* units mounted a number of raids against towns and harbours in the south of England. Repelling attacks by fighter-bomber Messerschmitts became a major headache for the British defences as the *Jabo* campaign continued. RAF Fighter Command units could not be scrambled quickly enough to intervene, and actually finding the fast, low-flying *Jabos* was, in any case, a major challenge even if defending aircraft could be vectored into the right areas. Ground- and ship-based anti-aircraft guns proved to be of greatest use in countering the marauding Messerschmitts, with even the humble Bren gun being effective in this regard.

ENHANCED CAPABILITY

Both 10./JG 2 and 10./JG 26 were brought together under the direction of *Luftflotte* 3. However, during June 1942, personnel of both *Staffeln* were gradually relocated from the frontline, although some operations continued. The reason for their removal was to re-equip the two dedicated Bf 109 *Jabo* units with the Fw 190, this process principally taking place at Le Bourget airfield just outside Paris.

The Bf 109 *Jabos* had done an effective job with the two *Staffeln* that flew the type up to that point in 1942, and had probably achieved considerably more than their comparatively small numbers would suggest. In effect, the Bf 109F had been an ad hoc stand-in until the clearly more capable *Jabo*-configured Fw 190 became available in sufficient numbers to take the operational capability of the small fighter-bomber arm significantly forward. Summing up the work of the diminutive *Jabo* force thus far, Generalmajor Osterkamp later wrote;

'The Me 109 was not made or at first intended for dropping bombs. Operational needs made it into a fighter that was also a bomber, but it was not an ideal change.'

In contrast, the Fw 190 was a versatile design capable of performing both the fighter and the fighter-bomber missions with ease. The initial fighter version, the Fw 190A-1, had started to reach operational capability with the Luftwaffe a year earlier, the first aircraft having been accepted by JG 26 on the Channel Front during the summer of 1941. Following transition training for some of the *Geschwader*'s pilots on the type at Le Bourget, operations began sporadically during August 1941, 6./JG 26 being the first to use the type on genuine fighter operations. At that time this *Staffel* was still flying the Bf 109F as its main equipment. The Focke-Wulf was therefore gradually eased into service, with other elements of JG 26 transitioning onto the Fw 190A fighter as more airframes became available. This *Geschwader* was joined as an Fw 190A fighter operator by JG 2 on the Channel Front in the following months.

Overall, the Fw 190 was a completely different, newer and more deadly warplane compared to the Bf 109F. By the time that dedicated *Jabo* examples of the Focke-Wulf became available to be flown operationally in the summer of 1942, the Fw 190A was already a proven fighter.

Up to that point the Bf 109F had been an effective fighter-bomber, although its shortcomings particularly in respect to range had been a significant factor in restricting its potential *Jabo* activities. The arrival on the Channel Front of the Fw 190 for fighter-bomber raids was a complete game changer. Very different to the Bf 109, the Focke-Wulf represented a major upgrade in the Luftwaffe's capabilities.

Compared to the Spitfire VB, which was then the pick of the RAF fighter types available to counter the *Jabo* threat on the Channel Front, the Fw 190A was superior in virtually every respect. Although the Spitfire could out-turn the German fighter, it was up to 30 mph slower – significantly for anti-*Jabo* operations, much of this speed deficit was at low-level, where the Spitfire VB would be expected to counter the fast Focke-Wulf fighter-bomber. The Fw 190 also had a much better rate of roll. With its air-cooled radial engine rather than the Bf 109F's liquid-cooled Daimler-Benz DB 601, with its vulnerable cooling system, the Fw 190's BMW 801 was less likely to succumb to battle damage – an ever-present danger when operating at low-level against heavily defended targets.

The first cross-Channel attack with the new Focke-Wulf *Jabos* was mounted by 10./JG 2 on 7 July 1942. It involved two aircraft which attacked shipping off the Isle of Wight, with claims being made for the damage or sinking of three small vessels. The longer range, faster and more powerful Fw 190A proved to be an immediate major step forward in capability for the *Jabo* pilots over the Bf 109F, and the aircraft was certainly capable of matching anything the RAF had available to counter it during that period.

Further sorties were flown on subsequent days by 10./JG 2. Amongst these was an attack against shipping west of Portland, in Dorset, on 9 July, a raid on Brixham harbour three days later and a further mission to Dartmouth, in Devon, on 13 July. The latter was a major success for the fledgling Fw 190A *Jabo* force. Although Dartmouth itself was shrouded in low cloud, the two attacking Focke-Wulfs chanced upon the Free French submarine chaser *Rennes* (CH 8), which was preparing to escort a submarine into harbour. Presumably using the 'Liesendahl Method', Leutnant Leopold Wenger succeeded in dropping his bomb onto the ship

The Free French submarine chaser *Rennes* (CH 8) was one of the first vessels to be sunk by Fw 190 *Jabos* on the Channel Front, the crew of the 107-ton warship being taken by surprise when two aircraft from 10./JG 2 attacked out of low cloud off Dartmouth on 13 July 1942. Leutnant Leopold Wenger successfully hit his target almost amidships with a single 250-kg bomb. The weapon destroyed the vessel, killing all bar one of its 28-man crew (*Tony Holmes Collection*)

almost amidships. This caused a huge explosion which destroyed the vessel, killing all bar one of its 28-man crew.

However, only a short time into the operational use of the *Jabo* Fw 190s, 10./JG 2 suffered a significant loss. After successfully perfecting many of the tactics used by the *Jabos* in the West, and surviving all through the Bf 109 period, Hauptmann Frank Liesendahl was shot down and killed. On 17 July 1942, he was part of a four-aircraft *Schwarm* that had sortied from Caen-Carpiquet. In the proximity of Berry Head near Brixham, the Focke-Wulf pilots attacked the small 1,128 gross ton coastal tanker SS *Daxhound* and its escort of two armed motor launches. The escorts accurately returned fire, with that from ML 118 being credited with causing one of the Fw 190s to crash into the sea. Liesendahl's body was discovered in the water off the Devon coast several weeks later, the veteran *Jabo* pilot having been lost while flying Fw 190A-2 Wk-Nr 120439 'Blue 14'.

The loss of Liesendahl right at the start of Fw 190 *Jabo* operations in the West was a huge blow to the small fighter-bomber force. However, as more Focke-Wulfs became available during the summer of 1942 for the *Jabo* pilots of both JGs 2 and 26, the type's obvious advantages over the Bf 109F became increasingly apparent.

Liesendahl was replaced as *Staffelkapitän* of 10./JG 2 by Oberleutnant Fritz Schröter, who had been in temporary charge of 10./JG 26 following the removal of Hauptmann Karl Plunser on 12 July 1942. The leadership of 10./JG 26 was taken over by Oberleutnant Joachim-Hans Geburtig. However, shortly thereafter on 30 July, Geburtig, with Feldwebel Emil Bösch, flew an anti-shipping mission from Caen-Carpiquet. While attacking a collier two miles southeast of Littlehampton, on the West Sussex coast, Geburtig's Fw 190A-3, Wk-Nr 137003 'Black 1', was hit by return fire from the small vessel and crashed into the water, the German pilot being picked up and taken prisoner. He was replaced by Leutnant Paul Keller, who was taken on as a *Staffelführer* rather than a full *Staffelkapitän*, the former title usually being reserved for less-experienced junior officers or temporary postings.

Amongst the earliest Focke-Wulf *Jabos* to see operational service were a selection of Fw 190A-2 and A-3 airframes configured as fighter-bombers before the main Fw 190A-4/U8 and A-5/U8 *Jabos* became available. They included this Fw 190A-2 (although it is sometimes referred to as an A-3) Wk-Nr 080 'Blue 6' of 10./JG 2. Based at Caen-Carpiquet in mid-1942, the aircraft – seen here jacked up for weapons adjustment – was flown by Leutnant Heinz Schumann, who later led the *Staffel* from December 1942 as an Oberleutnant (*Malcolm V Lowe Collection*)

The difficulties experienced by the British defences in countering the incoming fighter-bombers had led to increased patrols by locally based fighter units, and on 1 August one of these was successful. On that day, two Spitfire VBs of Canadian-manned No 412 Sqn based at RAF Merston, in West Sussex, were on patrol south of Shoreham-by-Sea, also in West Sussex, at 1000 ft. Incoming at 1000 hrs were Fw 190A fighter-bombers flown by Oberfeldwebel Karl-Heinz Knobeloch and Leutnant Arnd Flock of 10./JG 26. Canadian pilots Flg Off George Davidson and Plt Off Ken Robb spotted the two Focke-Wulfs and dived after them. A summary of the subsequent combat was written by the Sector Intelligence Officer at RAF Tangmere, in West Sussex;

'Yellow 1 [Davidson] closed to within 100 yards of the nearest e/a [enemy aircraft] apparently without being seen, firing a 2½ second burst of cannon and machine gun astern. Strikes were seen all over the e/a and black smoke was coming from the engine as it crashed sideways into the sea approximately 10–15 miles south of Brighton. Yellow 2 [Robb] reports that the e/a exploded on striking the sea, and afterwards dense smoke up to 300 ft and flame was seen for three or four minutes.'

Robb chased the second Focke-Wulf and achieved hits, but he could not verify if the aircraft escaped. It apparently returned home, damaged. The fighter-bomber that Davidson shot down was Fw 190A-2 Wk-Nr 125253 'White 5' of Leutnant Flock, who was killed. This was the first aerial victory claimed by RAF Fighter Command over the Fw 190 *Jabo* units in the West – a major success for the defenders.

Nevertheless, it was in August 1942 that the tactics and mission requirements of the two fighter-bomber *Staffeln* changed dramatically.

The famous *Staffel* emblem of 10./JG 2 featured a dark red/brown fox with a broken ship in its mouth – this insignia was allegedly designed by the fiancée of *Jabo* ace Oberleutnant Frank Liesendahl. It was initially applied to the unit's Bf 109F *Jabos* when 10./JG 2 was flying anti-shipping attacks off the south coast of England in 1941. The emblem was subsequently painted onto the engine cowlings of the *Staffel*'s Focke-Wulfs in the early months of their service on the Channel Front (*Malcolm V Lowe Collection*)

Although shipping and coastal towns still retained importance, the wily fighter-bombers were now tasked with striking at industrial and populated targets much further inland. True, both units had previously attempted to attack targets of this type while flying the Bf 109F, but the faster and longer-legged Fw 190A made the success of such raids much more of a possibility.

The first such low-level attack was carried out on 5 August when two *Jabos* from 10./JG 2 bombed the Somerset town of Yeovil. Home to Westland Aircraft, this location was a prime target for the Luftwaffe, although the attack paid no attention to the prominent aircraft factory and its adjacent airfield. Instead the two *Jabo* pilots, Unteroffizier Kurt Bressler and

One of the early *Jabo* raids carried out by 10./JG 2 with its new Focke-Wulfs was an attack on the Cornish town of Bodmin on 7 August 1942. Civilian areas were targeted by the four aircraft involved, causing nine deaths and considerable damage (*Andy Saunders Collection*)

Feldwebel Karl Blase, deliberately focused on the centre of the town, each dropping a single bomb and machine gunning civilians. It was reported in Germany that the raid was intended as a revenge attack in response to RAF Bomber Command's targeting of smaller German towns rather than the 'big city' raids of earlier that year. At least 15 buildings were destroyed and many more damaged, with three civilians killed and 25 injured. Both Focke-Wulfs escaped unscathed at low-level.

On 7 August a similar raid was carried out by four *Jabos* of 10./JG 2 against the Cornish town of Bodmin and the village of Constantine. A four-aircraft *Schwarm* was involved, forward operating for this attack from Morlaix, in Brittany, rather than the *Staffel*'s now established home of Caen-Carpiquet in Normandy. Again, the motive was retaliation for RAF Bomber Command raids, and civilian areas were not off limits for the attacking force. The centre of Bodmin was hard hit, with a residential area being struck by one of the bombs, killing nine civilians. A gas works was set on fire and one of the raiders also appears to have attempted to bomb Truro railway station.

Four days later, the cathedral city of Salisbury, in Wiltshire, was the target. Two Focke-Wulfs of 10./JG 2 were involved, temporarily forward-based at Cherbourg-Maupertus (also known to the Germans as Cherbourg-Théville and Cherbourg/Ost). Once more, the defences were caught out by the speed and low-level approach of the two *Jabos*, one of which successfully damaged the local gas works with machine-gun and cannon fire. Gas holders were a prominent British landmark in the early 1940s, proving to be both useful reference points and easy targets for attacking aircraft. On this occasion the bombs dropped did not cause civilian deaths.

The events of 19 August 1942 proved to be highly significant for the small Focke-Wulf *Jabo* force, and resulted in one of the most successful single actions of the war for the Fw 190 fighter-bombers in the West. Codenamed Operation *Jubilee*, the predominantly Canadian landings at Dieppe, on the northern French coast, by more than 6000 troops that day were a total disaster.

Principal amongst the Luftwaffe units involved in the German response were both 10./JG 2 and 10./JG 26. Although it has been

Leutnant Leopold Wenger flew several Focke-Wulf *Jabos* during his time with 10./JG 2 and, subsequently, IV./SKG 10, including this aircraft, believed to be Fw 190A-3 Wk-Nr 467 'Blue 12' of 10./JG 2. Wenger was eventually killed on 10 April 1945 in aerial combat with Soviet fighters over his native Austria (*Chris Goss Collection*)

claimed in subsequent years that the Do 217 twin-engined bombers of *Kampfgeschwadern* (KG) 2 and 40 inflicted significant losses on the landing force and its ships offshore, in fact it was the *Jabos* of JGs 2 and 26 that created considerable havoc amongst the Allied vessels. Experienced in anti-shipping strikes, the Focke-Wulf pilots proved deadly in this action, which was largely unexpected by the Germans.

An initial operation was flown from Caen-Carpiquet by 10./JG 2 pilots Unteroffizier Werner Magarin and Feldwebel Karl Blase during the morning. They attacked one of the warships offshore supporting *Jubilee*, although Magarin's Focke-Wulf was so badly damaged by anti-aircraft fire that the pilot was forced to make a crash-landing west of Dieppe at Paluel.

A second operation was mounted almost immediately after by the unit's *Staffelkapitän*, Oberleutnant Fritz Schröter, accompanied by Leutnante Gerhard Limberg and Erhard Nippa. They again attacked one of the warships offshore, claiming hits with all three of their bombs. A third mission from Caen, comprising Unteroffizier Walter Höfer, Leutnant Leopold Wenger and two unnamed pilots, attacked the invasion fleet at midday. Each of the four pilots dropped a single 500-kg bomb and then strafed landing craft. Unteroffizier Höfer also claimed to have shot down a Spitfire. At roughly the same time, 10./JG 26 flew a *Jabo* mission over the Dieppe area, although one of its escorting Fw 190A fighters from 2./JG 26 was shot down, its pilot being killed.

The fourth operation of the day mounted by 10./JG 2 proved to be the most destructive. It comprised four *Jabos* and was led by Oberleutnant Schröter, accompanied by Leutnant Wenger and two unnamed pilots. Flying into a curtain of anti-aircraft fire, the Focke-Wulfs again attacked shipping

Leutnant Leopold Wenger's most effective *Jabo* mission was flown during the early afternoon of 19 August 1942 in response to the Allied amphibious assault on Dieppe, codenamed Operation *Jubilee*. He succeeded in hitting the Hunt-Class destroyer HMS *Berkeley* (L17) with a 500-kg bomb, breaking the vessel's back and knocking out its steering. The warship was abandoned and eventually sunk by its sister-ship, HMS *Albrighton* (L12). Wenger had sunk the submarine chaser *Rennes* (CH 8) just a month earlier (*Tony Holmes Collection*)

offshore. Wenger succeeded in dropping his 500-kg bomb onto the Hunt-Class destroyer HMS *Berkeley* (L17), severely damaging the vessel. A second bomb also reportedly struck the ship or exploded nearby. One of the most important Royal Navy vessels involved in the Dieppe landing, *Berkeley* had been in the thick of the fighting from the start, providing shore bombardment and acting as a command post for some of the air controllers and observers committed to the action.

By the time 10./JG 2 had attacked the warship in the early afternoon, Allied forces were withdrawing due to the landings having failed, and *Berkeley* was one of the last to leave the Dieppe area, stopping to pick up wounded Canadian servicemen from another vessel. The direct hit that Wenger achieved at around 1318 hrs broke the back of the destroyer and wrecked its steering. The survivors abandoned ship and were lucky to be picked up by other retreating Allied vessels. *Berkeley* was subsequently sent to the bottom by two torpedoes from sister-ship HMS *Albrighton* (L12), the second of which caused the forward magazine to explode.

10./JG 2's fifth, and last, mission of the day saw five aircraft target retreating Allied ships and landing craft off Brighton, inflicting further destruction and casualties on some of the smaller vessels. These were the last of 44 sorties flown by pilots of 10./JG 2 and 10./JG 26 in nine recognised missions that day, which again proved the worth to the Luftwaffe of the two fighter-bomber units. For just one aircraft lost to enemy action, plus a second loss due to an operational accident, they had inflicted significant damage on the Allied ships supporting the Dieppe landings.

In less than two years, however, the tables were to be completely turned when, in June 1944, Operation *Overlord* saw Allied landings in Normandy that were of a completely different scale to *Jubilee*. While trying to respond to D-Day, Luftwaffe fighter-bomber pilots would face odds that were by then stacked irrevocably and fatally against them.

For the time being, however, the penny packet but often destructive daily Channel Front attacks against English coastal towns and local shipping continued. Following the Dieppe operations, a short subsequent break was ended with a raid against Bournemouth (then in Hampshire, but nowadays in Dorset) and Salcombe, in Devon, on 22 August. The following day, Swanage in Dorset was visited by two *Jabos* which appear to have targeted the local gas works.

During the morning of 26 August it was the turn of Eastbourne, in East Sussex, to be attacked. The two 10./JG 26 pilots involved were Oberfeldwebel Werner Kassa and Obergefreiter Richard Wittman. Once more the *Jabo* pilots achieved surprise with their fast and low approach across the Channel. One of the two bombs dropped hit an electricity generating station, putting it temporarily out of action until repairs could be made. The second bomb exploded in a residential area,

The unlucky 'Black 13' of Oberfeldwebel Werner Kassa from 10./JG 26. On 26 August 1942 he was shot down and killed by accurate light anti-aircraft fire while raiding Eastbourne in Fw 190A-2 Wk-Nr 080 (probably 122080, but sometimes identified as an A-3, as Wk-Nr blocks were similar for the two near-identical variants). This might have been the same aircraft originally coded 'Blue 6' of 10./JG 2 shown on page 21 (*Andy Saunders Collection*) causing the deaths of three civilians and injuring seven others.

As the two Focke-Wulfs banked over the town, they flew past Caffyns garages, which were being used to maintain military vehicles. The works therefore had a defensive light anti-aircraft Bren gun mounted on the roof of one of the company's buildings, the weapon being manned by Pvt E G Johnstone of the Canadian Seaforth Highlanders. As the two *Jabos* banked to starboard in front of him, his deflection shooting was without equal as he put several rounds into Kassa's aircraft. The Fw 190 continued to bank before crashing inverted into a ditch beside the road at Lottbridge Drove. Kassa was killed when his aircraft, Fw 190A-2 Wk-Nr 122080 'Black 13' hit the ground. German pilots were generally not superstitious, but in this case the number '13' was not a good omen.

When Pvt Johnstone briefly fired his Bren gun, War Reserve Constable Harry Etherington had had a grandstand view;

'I saw two FW 190s come in from the sea from the direction of Langney Point. I saw two bombs dropped. One 'plane then turned right and came over the gas works. A machine gun posted on the top of Caffyns works in Seaside opened fire, and I saw bullets entering the machine. It faltered, then turned completely upside down and crashed into the ditch bordering Lottbridge Drove about 50 yards from me.'

On 29 August Falmouth was raided and the small steamship *Jernfeld* sunk. Three days later, 10./JG 26 suffered a further combat loss when, during an attack on targets at Lydd and Dungeness, in Kent, one of the participating Focke-Wulfs apparently developed engine trouble that eventually forced its pilot, Oberfeldwebel Heinrich Wagner, to ditch in the Channel. He was drowned when the aircraft, Fw 190A-2 Wk-Nr 125315 'Black 4', immediately sank.

The outstanding success of Pvt Johnstone in shooting down Oberfeldwebel Kassa with his Bren gun while defending Eastbourne on 26 August was equalled during the early evening of 4 September when 10./JG 2 returned to the often attacked Torbay area of Devon. Six aircraft bombed and strafed a number of targets, including communications and civilian areas, killing at least two service personnel. A Focke-Wulf flown by Unteroffizier Walter Höfer, who, days earlier, had been active targeting warships off Dieppe, got too close to a lone Bren gunner on the cliff at Berry Head and was shot down. The *Jabo* (Fw 190A-3 Wk-Nr 132242) crashed onto a nearby beach at 1851 hrs and burnt out, Höfer being killed.

Two Czech pilots from Spitfire VB-equipped No 312 Sqn were duly scrambled from RAF Bolt Head, also in Devon. They tried to chase the remaining *Jabos* as they fled from Torbay at low-level, but the Germans managed to stay ahead of the RAF fighters and returned safely to their temporary forward operating location of Cherbourg-Maupertus. Overall,

On 4 September 1942 10./JG 2 attacked the Torquay/Torbay area, which was rapidly becoming one of the *Staffel*'s most visited targets. During the raid, Unteroffizier Walter Höfer's Fw 190A-3 Wk-Nr 132242 was hit by rounds fired from a lone Bren gunner on the cliff at Berry Head. The aircraft subsequently crashed onto a nearby beach at 1851 hrs and burnt out, Höfer being killed (*Andy Saunders Collection*)

the Spitfire VB was proving to be a less than adequate counter to the fast *Jabos*, with the type usually struggling to catch the Fw 190 at low level.

Nevertheless, a further loss for 10./JG 2 occurred on 17 September when two Focke-Wulfs attacked Bognor Regis, in West Sussex. One 500-kg bomb struck the rear of the West Parade Hotel, killing a civilian and injuring seven others. The second bomb holed an empty gas holder and then exploded on a bridge, destroying electricity cabling as well as gas and water pipes. But this time the aerial defences were more successful. Two Spitfire VBs of No 412 Sqn were rapidly scrambled from nearby RAF Tangmere, their pilots sitting at readiness in the aircrafts' cockpits. The two Canadian airmen, Plt Off Lloyd Powell and Flg Off Barry Needham, were vectored onto the fleeing Germans. Quickly finding the fighter-bombers, they chased them out to sea. A summary of the subsequent combat was written by the Sector Intelligence Officer at RAF Tangmere;

'After approximately 10–15 minutes, both pilots had closed the range to 250 yards and each attacked one e/a. Green 2 [Plt Off Powell] opened fire with cannon and machine gun from astern with a series of short bursts totalling ten seconds whilst closing to 150 yards. After his first burst, he saw light blue smoke coming from the starboard side of the engine of the e/a, which increased in volume, and strikes all over the fuselage and tailplane. After the fourth or fifth burst, the e/a started to take evasive action consisting of gentle weaving turns. Strikes on the fuselage and tail plane were seen during two further bursts. Before the last burst, the e/a straightened out and flew low over the water, and shortly after carried out a tight loop off the deck, reaching approximately 700 ft, and then dived into the sea without leaving any trace. At the top of the loop, the cockpit cover and what appeared to be armour plating came away from the e/a.'

The Focke-Wulf that Plt Off Powell had shot down was Fw 190A-2 Wk-Nr 215 flown by Unteroffizier Hans-Walter Wandschneider, who was listed by the Germans as 'missing'. Meanwhile, Green 1 (Flg Off Needham) had almost caught the second *Jabo*, flown by Leutnant Leopold Wenger. Although he was able to hit the German aircraft several times, Wenger escaped and nursed his damaged Focke-Wulf back to Caen-Carpiquet.

The south coast of England much further to the east was generally the preserve of the *Jabos* of 10./JG 26 from their Saint-Omer-Wizernes base. This unit was as busy as 10./JG 2, mounting a string of attacks during September and into October 1942. One of these, on 24 September, concentrated on Hastings, in East Sussex, which was known to the Germans to be a training centre for cadets at the start of their flight education prior to actually taking to the air. A large raid by *Jabo* standards was mounted in the early evening of the 24th, which concentrated on shipping, in addition to the training locations onshore. It resulted in the deaths of two trainees, with 27 injured. The civilian toll was much higher at 23 dead and dozens more injured.

Inexperience led to the loss of one of 10./JG 26's recently arrived pilots during an attack by four aircraft on RAF

Unwisely making a second run against his target on the morning of 10 October 1942, 10./JG 26's Unteroffizier Werner Schammert was shot down by light anti-aircraft fire. His aircraft, Fw 190A-3 Wk-Nr 130420 'Black 7', crashed into a house in Wellington Crescent, Ramsgate, and disintegrated, its engine coming to rest against nearby railings (*Andy Saunders Collection*)

Manston airfield and a gas works in the Margate area of Kent during the morning of 10 October. Unwisely, Unteroffizier Werner Schammert came back for a second run over the target, by which time the ground defences were ready. With his Focke-Wulf mortally hit by light anti-aircraft fire, the German pilot put his fighter-bomber into a climb and bailed out. The aircraft, Fw 190A-3 Wk-Nr 130420 BO+UT 'Black 7', crashed into 27 Wellington Crescent, Ramsgate, and was destroyed.

A further loss occurred exactly one week later, and it represented a new success for the coastal defences. On that day, 10./JG 26 again attacked Hastings, hitting a number of non-military locations including St Columba's Church and the adjacent Warrior Gardens. The church, originally built in the 1880s, was destroyed, and a large dwelling at 45 Pevensey Gardens was also hit. Two civilians were killed and 16 injured. However, as the *Jabos* fled the scene, they were chased by new, very powerful adversaries – Hawker Typhoons.

The Typhoon had started to enter RAF squadron service during late 1941, although the fighter was initially plagued by a number of problems primarily associated with its complicated Napier Sabre engine. Nevertheless, its useful turn of speed, especially at low level, made it a potentially deadly adversary to counter the Luftwaffe's 'hit and run' raids. Although less manoeuvrable than the Spitfire, the Typhoon was at least 40 mph faster than Mk VB at low level, which would therefore make all the difference in a chase against fast-flying Focke-Wulfs. It was also armed with heavier firepower than the Spitfire VB – four 20 mm Hispano cannon, two in each wing, these hard-hitting weapons giving the type a potentially formidable striking power against the Fw 190.

During the later summer/early autumn of 1942, several Typhoon units of RAF Fighter Command were assigned to intercept the *Jabos*, taking up residence at suitable locations. They were New Zealand-manned No 486 Sqn at RAF West Malling, in Kent (following a brief spell at RAF North Weald, in Essex), No 266 Sqn at RAF Warmwell, in Dorset, No 257 Sqn at RAF Exeter, in Devon, and No 609 Sqn at RAF Biggin Hill, also in Kent – there were subsequent relocations of these and other units. The squadrons began mounting standing patrols during daylight hours of two aircraft, with two more on the ground at 'cockpit readiness'.

On 17 October this new tactic paid off. A two-aircraft patrol by No 486 Sqn's Sgt Artie Sames and Plt Off Gordon Thomas was sufficiently near to Hastings to spot two 10./JG 26 Focke-Wulfs as they concluded their attack and made their escape. The Typhoon pilots gave chase, and a summary of their subsequent combat was written by the local Intelligence Officer at RAF West Malling;

'At 1425 hours, when flying east to west at 500 ft at about ½ mile inland, they observed two FW 190s flying roughly northeast over the sea at 20–30 ft and about 1½ miles ahead. Yellow 1 [Plt Off Thomas] saw a bomb burst in the town. The enemy aircraft then turned to port due south and out to sea, where they split up, one flying southeast at sea level and the other continuing south at about 20–30 ft, followed by Yellow Section flying at sea level.

'Yellow 1 opened fire at long range with several short bursts of cannon fire and noticed splashes in the sea short of the e/a, which immediately started to weave. Yellow Section closed to within 500 yards and the enemy aircraft began a spiral weave. Yellow 1 opened fire again with several more short bursts and observed strikes on the side of the fuselage. The e/a pulled up violently and then winged over to port and down to sea level right across Yellow 2's [Sgt Sames] line of fire, then straightened out and climbed up slowly. Yellow 2 fired three short bursts at 200–250 yards, striking the fuselage and engine. A jet of flames burst from the starboard side of the engine, the hood was jettisoned and parts of the aircraft fell away and it turned over and fell burning into the sea, disappearing immediately.'

The pilot of the downed aircraft was Feldwebel Hermann Niesel, who was killed. His Focke-Wulf, Wk-Nr 142403 'Black 14', was one of the newer Fw 190A-4 models. Interestingly, the 10./JG 26 report on this incident wrongly identified the British fighters as 'Curtiss Tomahawks'.

To the west, in the area that was mainly the preserve of 10./JG 2, attacks also continued. The unit mounted a four-aircraft *Schwarm* raid against Totnes, in Devon, on 21 October, dropping four bombs in and around the town centre. Two civilians and an RAF officer were killed and seven injured. On 25 October, Torquay was targeted once again – like Hastings, the Devonshire town was frequently raided by the *Jabos*. Four aircraft from 10./JG 2 were involved, with two of the four bombs dropped being targeted on nearby Babbacombe. The remaining two hit Torquay, causing considerable damage and loss of life.

One landed on, and the other near to, the Palace Hotel, which was being used as a hospital for RAF officers. Five hospital staff were killed together with 14 ranking RAF personnel, while another 30 officers and ten staff members were injured. Two men from the local Home Guard were also killed.

Although it was usual for the two Fw 190 *Jabo* squadrons to operate entirely independently, on 31 October a different type of raid was carried out. Intended as a revenge attack in reply to RAF Bomber Command's targeting of German cities, it was a maximum effort mission against Canterbury, in Kent, comprising both 10./JG 2 and 10./JG 26, in addition to a newcomer – III. *Gruppe* of *Zerstörergeschwader* (ZG) 2. This *Zerstörer* unit had formerly operated Bf 110 twin-engined heavy fighters in the Mediterranean, but it had relocated to Cognac, in southwestern France, during September 1942 to convert onto the Fw 190A for *Jabo* operations.

To further reinforce the Canterbury reprisal attack, several standard Fw 190As from II./JG 2 became impromptu fighter-bombers for the raid. The exact number of *Jabos* that took part is thus hard to verify, but it appears to have been in the region of 30 – a very large number compared to the more usual fighter-bomber operations totalling two or four aircraft.

The attack took place on the evening of 31 October, with 10./JG 2 and III./ZG 2 using Merville in northeast France, some 19 miles west of Lille,

The Focke-Wulf *Jabos* of 10./JG 26, like those of 10./JG 2, featured a 'chevron and bar' marking on their rear fuselages, although the former turned the 'bar' into a stylised bomb motif as seen here. This Fw 190A-5/U8 of 10./JG 26 was photographed taxiing out at Saint-Omer-Wizernes carrying an SC 500 bomb (*Malcolm V Lowe Collection*)

as their temporary forward base. Take-off was at approximately 1740 hrs local time, the *Jabos* forming up over Calais and meeting their escort of Fw 190A fighters from JGs 2 and 26 before proceeding across the Channel at wave-top height. Although the British defences claimed to have given Canterbury residents notification of their approach, some had already heard false alarm air raid warnings earlier in the day and so the arrival of the fighter-bombers caught many off-guard. Bombs were dropped across several areas of Canterbury, causing considerable damage to mainly civilian locations and killing at least 29, with 95 injured.

The local light anti-aircraft defences shot down Feldwebel Alfred Hell of 5./JG 2, the impromptu fighter-bomber pilot bailing out of his stricken Fw 190A-2 Wk-Nr 125250 'Black 2' and being taken prisoner. As the *Jabos* fled the scene, they were intercepted by a number of RAF Spitfires and Typhoons from several units, but the apparently inexperienced defenders suffered several losses. Indeed, an arriving No 609 Sqn Typhoon was shot down by a Spitfire VB from No 122 Sqn. The only German casualty during these post-strike air battles was 8./JG 26's Leutnant Paul Galland, younger brother of Generalmajor Adolf Galland, who was killed flying his Fw 190A-4 Wk-Nr 142402 'Black 1'. He probably fell victim to the Spitfire VB flown by French pilot Sqn Ldr Jean-François Demozay, CO of No 91 Sqn based at RAF Hawkinge, in Kent.

Encouraged by their success in the Canterbury raid, the newly arrived *Jabos* of III./ZG 2 mounted a raid of their own on 3 November against Newton Abbot, in Devon. The four aircraft involved were from 8./ZG 2, but instead of flying against this Devonshire town they bombed Teignmouth on the Devon coast instead, two of the four then machine-gunning the village of Maidencombe. As the *Schwarm* of Focke-Wulfs headed back across the Channel, two Typhoons of No 257 Sqn detached to RAF Bolt Head were scrambled. Flg Off Geoffrey Ball's combat report stated;

'I was leader of Blue Section on standby at Bolt Head and we were scrambled on a vector of 120 degrees. We actually flew on 140 degrees for three minutes and then turned onto 120 degrees for five minutes. My Number 2 [Plt Off Peter Scotchmer] heard the controller transmitting so we pulled up from sea-level to 1000 ft to hear the message "Aircraft to starboard". I weaved to starboard and to port and saw four FW 190s in wide line abreast at sea level heading south three to four miles in front of me. I told my Number 2 "12 o'clock" and we dived in a right-hand turn, coming in two miles behind them at sea level

'After a six-minute chase at 360 IAS [indicated airspeed], I was in range of the outside left e/a, which made gentle turns to port and starboard as if undecided as to what evasive action to take. At 300 yards I fired a four-second burst from astern to ten degrees deflection. After strikes and a flash on the starboard side of the cockpit and engine, I saw a column of smoke and pieces flying off the aircraft as it hit the sea.

'I pulled up to starboard after another e/a which I lost sight of through my widescreen being misted up. I started to chase the fourth e/a, but thinking that the other two were behind me, I turned to see where they were and saw wreckage of my e/a on the water and a burning oil patch from the e/a shot down by my Number 2. As the fourth e/a was a long way ahead and nearly over the French coast and the third e/a was lost in cloud, I told my Number 2 to return to base independently.'

The two German pilots shot down at approximately 1210 hrs were Unteroffizier Johann Hannig in Fw 190A-2 Wk-Nr 120503 'Black 6' and Leutnant Hermann Kenneweg in Fw 190A-3 Wk-Nr 132150 'Black 3'. Both were killed. III./ZG 2 apparently played no further part in operations on the Channel Front, commencing a move to North Africa later that month.

On 4 November, the leadership of 10./JG 26 was assumed by Oberleutnant Kurt Müller. Later that month the *Jabos* of both 10./JG 2 and 10./JG 26 were detached to Istres-le Tubé northwest of Marseille, in southern France, as a response to the Allied landings in North Africa (Operation *Torch*) which took place on 8 November 1942. 10./JG 2 departed Caen-Carpiquet on 9 November, with 10./JG 26 leaving Saint-Omer-Wizernes on 14 November.

While they were away, some *Jabo* missions were mounted by normal fighter squadrons. Taking the form of 'nuisance' raids rather than actual *Jabo* operations, they were performed without bombs. Named *Störangriff* and *Tiefangriff*, they were small-scale strafing attacks that nevertheless could be deadly. But the German pilots involved were obviously not experienced or had not been trained in low-level operations, resulting in several losses. On 29 November, Ashford, in Kent, was targeted by JG 26. Oberfeldwebel Heinrich Bierwith of 5./JG 26 attacked a small locomotive, but he was too low and struck the engine's steam dome. The resulting explosion of steam caused the Focke-Wulf to crash, killing the pilot.

The next day, two fighters of 4./JG 26 attacked RAF Exeter and then split up. One aircraft flew along the coast near Teignmouth at low level and then crashed into the sea. The other attempted to attack shipping off Berry Head, including the armed trawler HMT *Finesse*, whose gunner, Seaman Jenkins, claimed to have shot the aircraft down with two short five-round bursts from his 'ancient' Hotchkiss 0.303-in. machine gun – the crew of the vessel's Oerlikon 20 mm cannon also fired at the Fw 190. Both pilots, Leutnante Roland Prym and Wilhelm Cadenbach, were killed. On 7 December a Focke-Wulf of 1./JG 26 flown by Obergefreiter Willi Muskatewitz crashed into Oxendean Hill, East Sussex, killing the pilot.

Despite the presence in the south of France of the potent fighter-bombers of 10./JG 2 and 10./JG 26, no operational sorties were flown by them against the Allied forces of Operation *Torch*, and the fear of a possible invasion on the southern French coast did not materialise. In mid-December the detachment was stood down and the aircraft were flown back to Caen-Carpiquet and Saint-Omer-Wizernes, respectively. This allowed 10./JG 2 to fly its first *Jabo* mission for several weeks on 14 December when military installations in the vicinity of the British Army's Lulworth ranges in Dorset were bombed by two Focke-Wulfs.

The first operation for 10./JG 26 following its return from the south of France was mounted on 19 December when Sandwich,

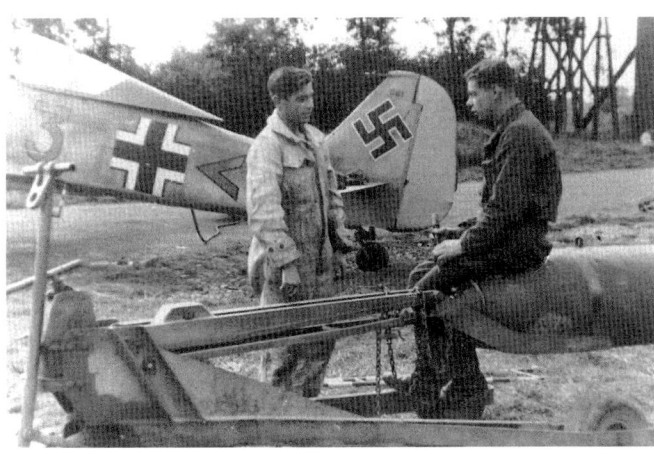

A 250-kg bomb attached to a wheeled carry cradle serves as a useful perch for a groundcrewman in discussion with a fellow maintainer from 10./JG 2, with what is thought to be Fw 190A-2 Wk-Nr 081 (probably 122081) 'Blue 3' in the background. The photograph was taken at the unit's base of Caen-Carpiquet, which was considerably expanded by the Germans following its capture in June 1940 to become one of the main Focke-Wulf *Jabo* airfields on the Channel Front (*Chris Goss Collection*)

in Kent, was bombed by four Focke-Wulfs. As the German aircraft fled the scene, they were intercepted by Typhoons of No 609 Sqn. Belgian pilot Flg Off Raymond Lallemant caught and claimed the destruction of one of the *Jabos*, which had apparently also been fired at and probably hit by the ground defences. Recently appointed *Staffelkapitän* Oberleutnant Kurt Müller was killed, his aircraft being Fw 190A-4 Wk-Nr 712 'White 9'. His replacement was Oberleutnant Paul Keller, who had previously led 10./JG 26 prior to Müller taking charge.

A number of raids were carried out in the closing days of December 1942, the attack against Eastbourne on the 29th once more leading to destruction in residential areas – two people were killed and at least 33 injured. The mission was undertaken by stand-in *Jabos* from 8./JG 2, the two aircraft involved being led by that unit's *Staffelkapitän*, Oberleutnant Bruno Stolle. A seasoned fighter pilot, Stolle attacked two patrolling Spitfire VBs of No 91 Sqn that the Focke-Wulfs came across while making their escape, successfully shooting down one of them.

JABO SCHOOLING

Training for the personnel of the frontline *Jabo* squadrons was carried out at Cognac during 1942 and into early 1943 by I./*Kampfschulgeschwader* (KSG) 3. Some of the pilots selected for *Jabo* work had no prior experience of aerial combat, while others had spent some time on operations but not necessarily in the Fw 190.

When aviators were posted to Cognac they were initially schooled in a short course regarding fighter tactics, which included aerobatics in a Bücker Bü 133 Jungmeister advanced biplane trainer. Formation flying and aerobatic proficiency became an important part of the training, together with air-to-ground firing in the Fw 190. Once this was achieved, it was followed by bombing training, including briefing on attacks against land and sea targets. The airfield at Cognac was well-appointed, and it even had a nearby bombing range. Pilots were therefore able to practise the specific art of flying fighter-bomber sorties, while the good weather in southern France allowed tuition even during the winter months. Cognac was also well out of the way of Allied aerial activity.

On 1 February 1943, there was a reshuffle of training units which saw III. *Gruppe* of KG 101 formed at Cognac from I./KSG 3. It was commanded by Hauptmann Horst Beeger, who headed the *Gruppe* throughout its subsequent comparatively short existence. Within the new III./KG 101, its 7. (formerly 1./KSG 3) and 8. (formerly 2./KSG 3) *Staffeln* were also established on 1 February. 9. *Staffel* came from a different route, being created out of a part of *Erprobungstaffel* 410 on 6 June 1943. Never a particularly large unit, the *Gruppe* had 19 Fw 190A-3s, A-4s and A-5s assigned on 31 May 1943. Twelve of the aircraft were serviceable, shared between the 36 pilots then allocated to the unit.

Like I./KSG 3, III./KG 101 specifically trained *Jabo* pilots. On 14 July 1943 7./KG 101 was transferred from Cognac to Lechfeld, in Germany, where 9. *Staffel* had been based since its creation – the latter had been redesignated 13./KG 2 on 19 June. Eventually, during August 1943, III./KG 101 was disbanded.

CHAPTER THREE

THE CAMPAIGN CONTINUES

For the British defences, the 20 January 1943 *Jabo* raid on London was a total disaster, with many civilian casualties. Only one of the attacking Focke-Wulfs was shot down, Fw 190A-4/U8 Wk-Nr 142409 'Black 2' of 10./JG 26's Leutnant Hermann Hoch. He crash-landed near Capel, in Surrey, and destroyed the remains of his fighter-bomber with an explosive charge (*Andy Saunders Collection*)

The New Year of 1943 saw no let up in the *Jabo* attacks on southern England, which actually increased in their ferocity and intensity. Still comparatively small in number, the fighter-bomber pilots involved were nonetheless now well-versed in the necessary operating tactics and techniques associated with profitable fast, low-level fighter-bomber missions.

On 2 January the first *Jabo* attack off the year saw four aircraft from 10./JG 26 bomb Bexhill, in East Sussex. Several hours later, during the early afternoon, no fewer than eight Focke-Wulfs of 10./JG 2 targeted Kingsbridge, in Devon. The next day the same pattern was repeated, 10./JG 2 singling out Shanklin, on the Isle of Wight, and 10./JG 26 visiting Folkestone, on the Kent coast. This time the latter town was bombed from 16,000 ft, which was unusually high for a fighter-bomber raid.

The first loss of 1943 took place on 4 January when 10./JG 26 attacked Winchelsea, in East Sussex. Once again, anti-aircraft fire (on this occasion by members of the Royal Welsh Fusiliers) from strategically placed gun emplacements proved its worth. Fw 190A-4 Wk-Nr 142439 'Black 4' of Feldwebel Herbert Müller received multiple hits and, presumably disabled, impacted power lines. The aircraft crashed at Castle Farm, Winchelsea, at 1256 hrs, killing the pilot.

Four days later, Torquay was bombed yet again by 10./JG 2 when eight Focke-Wulfs hit a number of targets that included the Palace Hotel. On this occasion there were no recorded casualties.

On 10 January, an accurate and devastating attack was made on the often-visited port town of Teignmouth. Like a number of south coast locations such as Hastings, Eastbourne and Torquay, Teignmouth was a prime target due to its port facilities and light industry, much of which was helping the war effort to one extent or another. The town was also easy to find due to its distinctive layout and topography, with the local landmark cliffs, dubbed 'the Parson and Clerk' by residents, being particularly easy to identify. According to local historians, the town suffered 21 air raids during the war, with at least 79 people being killed.

The seven Focke-Wulfs that reached Teignmouth on the 10th flew along the coast, approaching from the southeast. Two attacked the harbour area and five bombed the town itself, which was of no military value whatsoever. This inflicted substantial damage on Teignmouth and killed a number of civilians, the destruction caused by the bombs being compounded by machine gun and cannon fire.

However, despite the damage and loss of life, on this occasion the standing patrols of RAF fighters were successful. Typhoon-operating No 266 Sqn based at RAF Exeter was putting up a number of two-aircraft flights guarding the Devon coast, and the pairing of Plt Off Sam Blackwell and Flg Off John Small became airborne at 1415 hrs and routed towards Exmouth. Spotting the formation of Focke-Wulfs during their attack, both pilots watched them turning to flee for safety across the Channel. Although outnumbered, the Typhoon pilots immediately gave chase. The excellent turn of speed of their aircraft proved decisive, allowing Plt Off Blackwell to pursue a group of three aircraft. Having gradually gained on them, he engaged the fighter-bombers, as he later noted in his combat report;

'I chased these and closed to within what I estimated to be 500 yards of one. I gave short continuous bursts and saw strikes on both fuselage and wings. One cannon jammed, which made accurate shooting difficult. Visibility out to sea was not good, and I gave up the chase, having spent all my ammunition.'

He had probably engaged Fw 190A-3 Wk-Nr 467 'Blue 12' of Leutnant Leopold Wenger, which returned to Caen-Carpiquet with a large hole in its starboard wing. Flg Off Small was more successful;

'[We] about turned [just short of Exmouth], and after flying for two minutes sighted eight [sic] aircraft low on the water, my height being about 300 ft, heading for what I thought was Torquay. Immediately reported e/a to Controller and my number 2 after opening throttle fully and increasing revs also fully. E/a were flying fairly close line abreast. One section nearest coast being slightly apart from main formation. I closed quite quickly on e/a, being just about 250 yards behind aircraft I had decided to attack, it being the innermost one of the outer section.

'As they reached the coast, I saw bomb strikes in the water and one burst on houses on the waterfront. Flak was quite intense and all over the place, heavy bursts were behind and to port. I gave one fairly long burst crossing waterfront and over town, bead being on fields behind the town. E/a turned to starboard, gave another burst throttling back as range was fast decreasing. As e/a was crossing coast gave final burst at about 100 yards range, saw flashes on aircraft and one very bright flash indeed from about the cockpit. E/a nosed down, still turning to starboard, I kept firing and it struck the sea some 30 to 50 yards ahead and 300 to 500 yards offshore. I had no time to evade cascade of water and debris that came up and felt a decided jar.

'On pulling out I saw an aircraft to port at about 600 ft. I gave chase, saw splash of water and thought it had jettisoned bomb. Caught this aircraft some ten miles offshore and was about to fire when I recognised it to be a Spitfire which had jettisoned long-range tanks.'

The Spitfire belonged to Czech-manned No 310 Sqn, which was based at RAF Exeter and whose pilots were searching for the Focke-Wulfs, although they made no known interceptions for this raid. The German who Flg Off Small shot down at 1435 hrs was Feldwebel Joachim von Bitter, whose *Jabo* (Fw 190A-3 Wk-Nr 135424) went into the water some 500 yards offshore from 'the Parson and Clerk', the pilot being killed.

Yet another attack was made against Eastbourne on 15 January by four aircraft of 10./JG 2, the early afternoon incursion resulting in seven civilian deaths and 38 injured. The Focke-Wulfs again fled the target at low level and successfully escaped interception.

Although the introduction of the Typhoon into the war against these totally indiscriminate German raids had given the RAF a potent opponent to the Fw 190 *Jabos*, in almost every case they were only able to engage with the raiders after they had dropped their bombs and strafed the local population. During the Battle of Britain the Chain Home radar system had effectively given early warning of incoming raids, allowing RAF fighters to be positioned so as to engage the incoming bombers before they reached their targets, but often these had been medium-level attacks that radar could easily pick up.

By early 1943 there was still no effective comprehensive radar coverage available to detect fast incoming *Jabos* flying at very low-level over the water of the English Channel, although a related system called Chain Home Low (CHL) was operational. On the Isle of Wight, a significant radar installation was codenamed 'Blackgang', but in many cases the first time that the local population became aware that they were being attacked was when the bombs began to fall. Often, the air raid warning sirens were too late to announce the presence of incoming raiders, with some only being sounded after the attack had taken place.

MANY CASUALTIES

And then, on 20 January, complete disaster struck. In retaliation for recent RAF Bomber Command raids on Berlin, a *Jabo* attack in force was successfully carried out against London. It was the first large-scale raid on the capital by the Luftwaffe's *Jabos* since the Battle of Britain period. Focke-Wulfs from both 10./JG 2 and 10./JG 26 were involved, using Abbeville-Drucat as their take-off airfield due to the numbers involved.

The objective was London itself, and the attacking force included Bf 109Gs configured as fighter-bombers from the *Einsatzstaffel (Jabo)* of *Jagdgruppe Süd*, normally based at Saintes in southwestern France. They had deployed to Abbeville-Drucat for the raid, their job being to launch a diversionary attack on Tunbridge Wells in Kent. They were joined by several experienced pilots from *Jagdgruppe Ost*, this separate formation being escorted by Fw 190 fighters. In addition, a further 29 Fw 190 fighters would carry out a diversionary fighter sweep east of the Thames Estuary and then cover the retreat of the main force of Fw 190 *Jabos* after they had attacked the capital. They were joined by ten new pressurised Bf 109G-1 fighters, which would provide top cover for the whole enterprise. These had been taken on charge by 6./JG 26 only weeks before, and the raid was to be their first major operation.

Ironically, the day began badly for the Germans. A two-aircraft weather reconnaissance was flown by Fw 190 fighters of 8./JG 26 at 0848 hrs. They were intercepted by two Typhoons of No 609 Sqn, one of which was flown by Flg Off Raymond Lallemant. He had successfully engaged the *Jabo* of 10./JG 26's recently appointed *Staffelkapitän*, Oberleutnant Kurt Müller, on 19 December. Lallemant duly shot down one of the two 8./JG 26 fighters, killing Leutnant Hans Kümmerling.

Despite this setback, the first *Jabos* took off from Abbeville at 1150 hrs, two 10./JG 2 aircraft flying a diversionary raid against Ventnor, on the Isle of Wight. At midday the main force started to take off, the London formation comprising 28 Fw 190s of both 10./JG 2 and 10./JG 26. The Bf 109 diversionary attack apparently became disorientated, losing sight of Tunbridge Wells and instead dropping bombs on Lewes, in East Sussex, where two civilians were killed and 45 injured.

But the main force precisely carried out their orders. Around 30 minutes after taking off, they arrived completely unchallenged over southeast London. With the local balloon barrage taken down for lunchtime, the *Jabos* attacked at will, dropping their bombs in a variety of locations. Although one bomb hit the Royal Naval College at Greenwich, and a power station was also targeted, the majority fell in civilian areas. Tragically, one of the locations was Sandhurst School in Catford, which received a direct hit. With only a last-minute air raid warning, none of the children had been able to reach the shelters, resulting in 38 being killed in addition to five of their teachers. The Focke-Wulfs then turned for home, exiting over Croydon, where children playing in Ashburton Park were strafed. Altogether, a further 26 civilians were killed additional to the fatalities at Sandhurst School, with many more injured.

The 'tail-end Charlie' of the London raid was the only casualty of the attack force. With his aircraft (Fw 190A-4/U8 Wk-Nr 142409 'Black 2') having been damaged by ground fire, Leutnant Hermann Hoch crash-landed near Capel, in Surrey. Uninjured, he was able to destroy the remains of the fighter-bomber with an explosive charge before being taken prisoner.

It was only when the *Jabos* were on their way home that the RAF was able to intervene. The aircraft of both 10./JG 2 and 10./JG 26 escaped, but their fighter escort and the diversionary Bf 109 *Jabos* suffered several losses – pilots of No 609 Sqn again proved the worth of their Typhoons. Altogether, at least ten German aircraft were shot down by Typhoons and Spitfires, with seven pilots killed and three taken prisoner. Three RAF fighters were in turn lost – two Spitfires and a Mustang I of Canadian-manned No 400 Sqn, the latter being mistaken for a German aircraft and downed by a Typhoon of No 486 Sqn. (*Text continues on page 48*)

COLOUR PLATES

1
Fw 190A-2 Wk-Nr 299 'Blue 2' + 'Chevron and Bar' of 10.(*Jabo*)/JG 2, Caen-Carpiquet, France, August 1942

2
Fw 190A-2 Wk-Nr 122080 'Black 13' + 'Chevron and Bomb' of Oberfeldwebel Werner Kassa, 10.(*Jabo*)/JG 26, Saint-Omer-Wizernes, France, August 1942

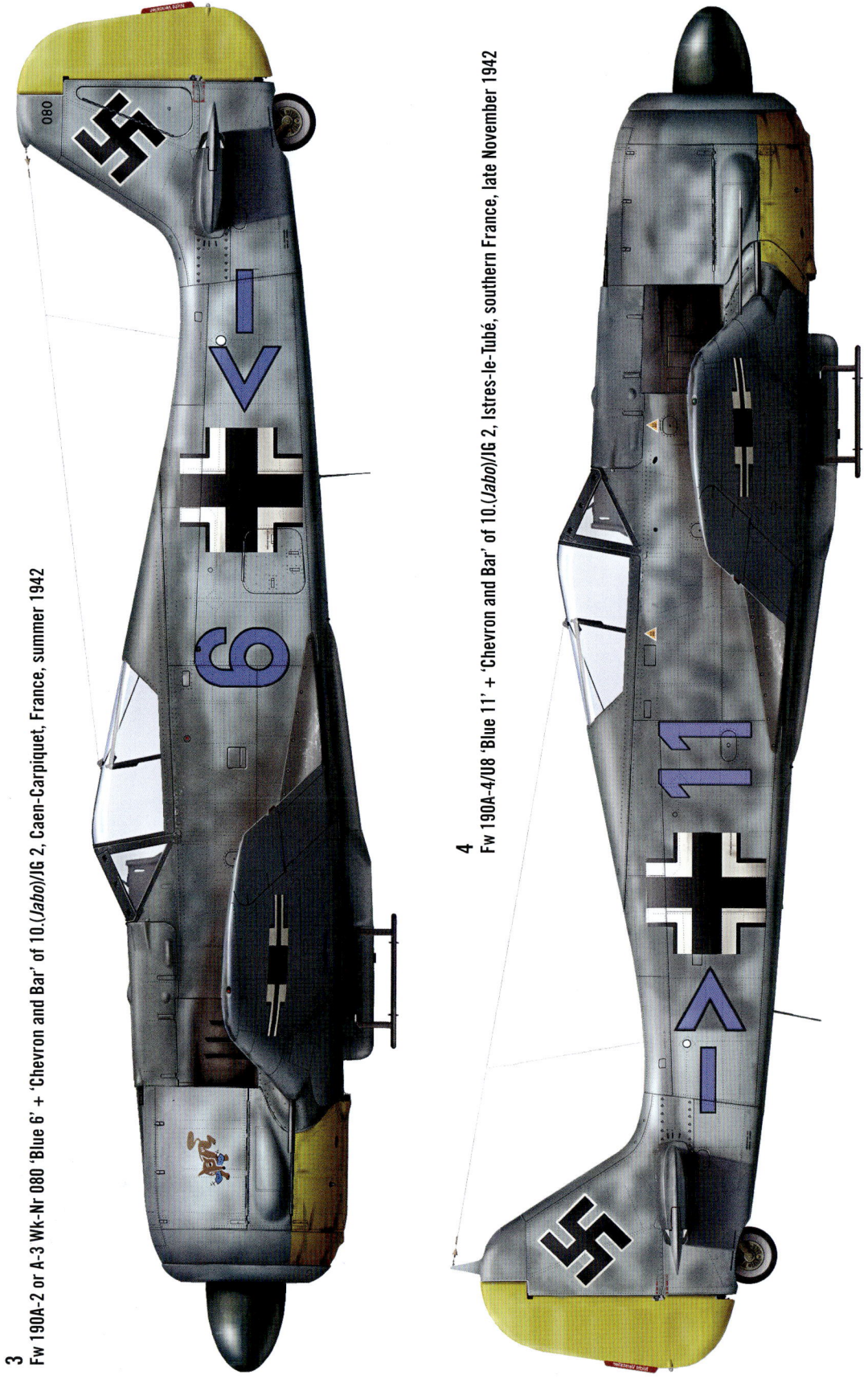

3
Fw 190A-2 or A-3 Wk-Nr 080 'Blue 6' + 'Chevron and Bar' of 10.(*Jabo*)/JG 2, Caen-Carpiquet, France, summer 1942

4
Fw 190A-4/U8 'Blue 11' + 'Chevron and Bar' of 10.(*Jabo*)/JG 2, Istres-le-Tubé, southern France, late November 1942

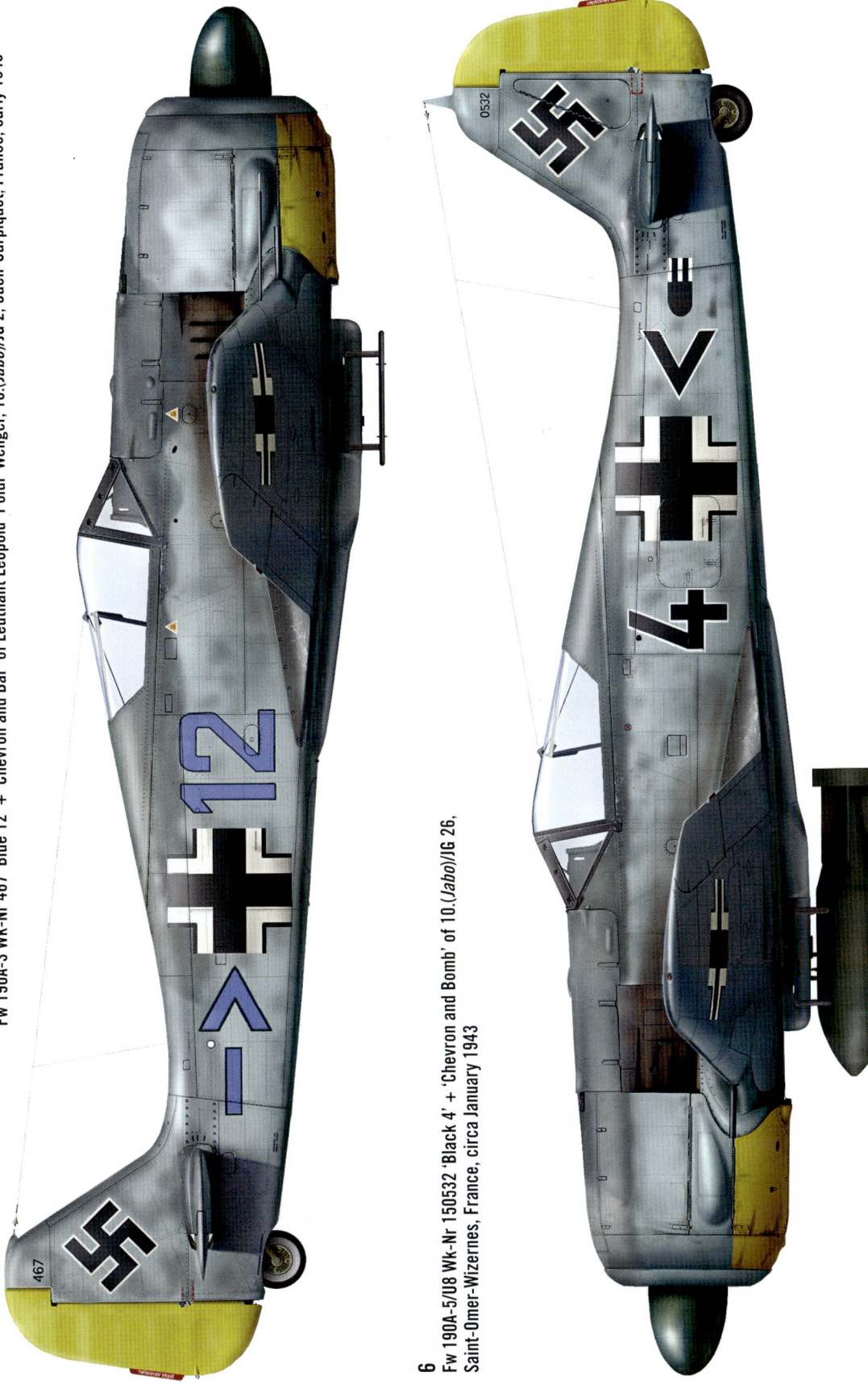

5
Fw 190A-3 Wk-Nr 467 'Blue 12' + 'Chevron and Bar' of Leutnant Leopold 'Poldi' Wenger, 10.(*Jabo*)/JG 2, Caen-Carpiquet, France, early 1943

6
Fw 190A-5/U8 Wk-Nr 150532 'Black 4' + 'Chevron and Bomb' of 10.(*Jabo*)/JG 26, Saint-Omer-Wizernes, France, circa January 1943

7
Fw 190A-4/U8 Wk-Nr 142409 'Black 2' + 'Chevron and Bomb' of Leutnant Hermann Hoch, 10.(Jabo)/JG 26, Abbeville-Drucat, France, 20 January 1943

8
Fw 190A-5/U8 'Black Triangle' + 'White 1' of II./SKG 10, Caen-Carpiquet, France, March 1943

9
Fw 190A-4/U8 Wk-Nr 147155 'Yellow H' of Feldwebel Otto Bechtold, 7./SKG 10, Amiens-Glisy, April 1943

10
Fw 190A-4/U8 Wk-Nr 147155 'Yellow H' of Feldwebel Otto Bechtold, 7./SKG 10, RAF West Malling, Kent, 17 April 1943

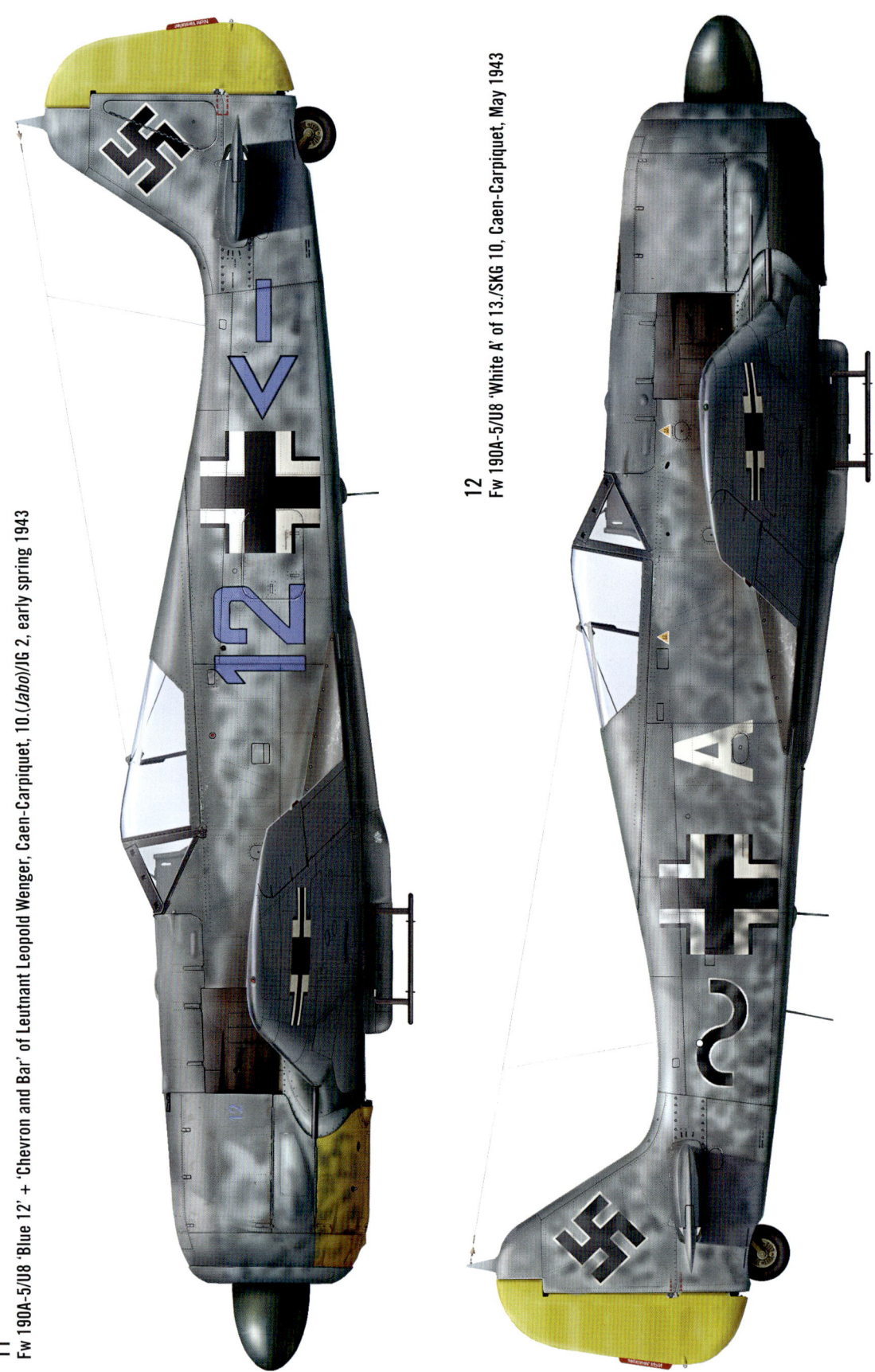

11
Fw 190A-5/U8 'Blue 12' + 'Chevron and Bar' of Leutnant Leopold Wenger, Caen-Carpiquet, 10.(*Jabo*)/JG 2, early spring 1943

12
Fw 190A-5/U8 'White A' of 13./SKG 10, Caen-Carpiquet, May 1943

13
Fw 190A-5/U8 'White E' of Leutnant Leopold Wenger, Caen-Carpiquet, 13./SKG 10, 23 May 1943

14
Fw 190A-4/U8 Wk-Nr 145843 'Red 9' of Unteroffizier Heinz Ehrhardt, 2./SKG 10, Caen-Carpiquet, France, May 1943

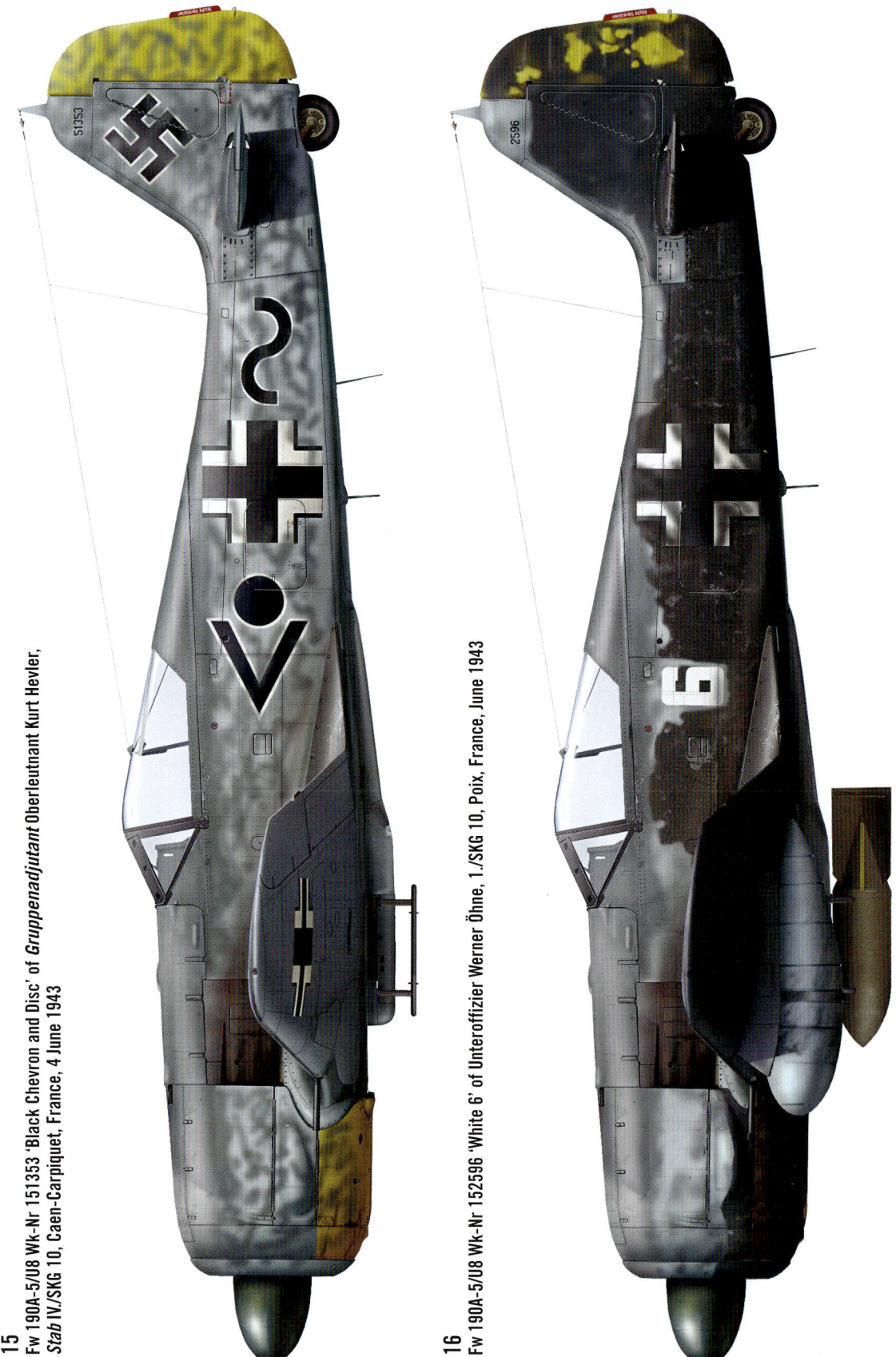

15
Fw 190A-5/U8 Wk-Nr 151353 'Black Chevron and Disc' of *Gruppenadjutant* Oberleutnant Kurt Hevler, *Stab* IV./SKG 10, Caen-Carpiquet, France, 4 June 1943

16
Fw 190A-5/U8 Wk-Nr 152596 'White 6' of Unteroffizier Werner Öhne, 1./SKG 10, Poix, France, June 1943

17
Fw 190G-3 'White 9' of 1./SKG 10, Normandy, France, June 1944

18
Fw 190F-8 'Brown 0' + 'Brown I' of 9./SG 4, Avord, France, summer 1944

19
Fw 190A-4/U8 PE882 (formerly Wk-Nr 147155 'Yellow H') of No 1426 (Enemy Aircraft) Flight, RAF Collyweston, Northamptonshire, October 1944

20
Fw 190D-9 Wk-Nr 210194 'Black Chevron and Bars' of Feldwebel Werner Hohenberg, *Stab* I./JG 2, Merzhausen, Germany, 1 January 1945

21
Fw 190A-8/R2 Wk-Nr 681497 'White 11' of Gefreiter Walter Wagner, II.(*Sturm*)/JG 4, Darmstadt-Griesheim, Germany, 1 January 1945

22
Fw 190A-8/R2 1-I-45 00-L (formerly Wk-Nr 681497 'White 11') of the 404th FG, A92 St Trond, Belgium, early 1945

This major action was a resounding success for the Fw 190 *Jabos*, and it had repercussions in Britain. The complete failure of the defences to prevent the raid became the subject of a Parliamentary debate – the first of its kind – and resulted in a petition by local residents. But a further disaster for the defences followed only three days later.

Four Focke-Wulfs of 10./JG 26 intended to perform a morning attack against Hailsham, in Sussex, on 23 January. Once more, there was no warning of the incoming raiders, although they failed to strike at their specified target. Instead, they unloaded their ordnance on the small town of Polegate some five miles north of Eastbourne, where three civilians were killed and six injured. They then continued on to Eastbourne itself, strafing the Old Town district. However, fleeing the scene at very low level put one of the Focke-Wulfs in the line of fire of two Bren guns at Beachy Head manned by Pvts Jack Andros and Carl Darroch of the Princess Patricia's Canadian Light Infantry. They raked the Focke-Wulf with Bren gun fire and the *Jabo* (Fw 190A-4/U8 Wk-Nr 145636 'Black 14') dived into the sea at Cow Gap, killing Unteroffizier Alfred Immervoll.

More misfortune befell the south of England's civilian population on 26 January when eight Focke-Wulfs of 10./JG 2 planned to raid the Devon town of Kingsbridge once again. Instead, the afternoon attack was carried out against the village of Aveton Gifford to the northwest of Kingsbridge, which had no military connection whatsoever. Seven bombs were dropped in and around the village, one striking and almost completely demolishing the local St Andrew's Church, the area then being strafed. Another bomb hit and destroyed the Rectory near to the church, killing five-year-old Sonia Weeks. Almost all the buildings in the village were damaged, and 20 local residents injured. Two Typhoons of No 266 Sqn were scrambled and headed for Start Point, southeast of Kingsbridge. Flg Off Clive Bell later wrote;

'While approximately halfway there, I sighted an FW 190 at 2 o'clock about 1,500 yards from me. I immediately "Tally Ho'd" over the R/T [radio telephone], gave chase and slowly closed the range to what I imagine must have been about 500 yards, as my first burst fell in the water about 15 yards behind the e/a. My next burst appeared to be very slightly in front, the e/a being so low that it actually flew through the spray sent up by the cannon shells. I think I probably first hit it then. The next burst hit it fair and square and bits flew off it and smoke poured from it. The e/a then pulled up very suddenly and steeply and I gave it one short final burst, after which it plunged into the sea. I then pulled up in a climbing turn to the left to avoid the shower of spray and bits which came up after the e/a had hit the water.'

The chase had taken the two aircraft some 12 miles out to sea, the Focke-Wulf (Fw 190A-4 Wk-Nr 145680 'Blue 7') being flown by Feldwebel Karl Blase. One of the more experienced *Jabo* pilots of 10./JG 2, he did not survive being shot down.

On 23 January 1943, four Fw 190A-4/U8 *Jabos* of 10./JG 26 were briefed to attack Hailsham, in East Sussex, but instead they bombed Polegate and then continued to Eastbourne. While exiting near Beachy Head to flee for home, the Focke-Wulf flown by Unteroffizier Alfred Immervoll (pictured) was shot down by Pvts Jack Andros and Carl Darroch of the Princess Patricia's Canadian Light Infantry, both of whom were manning Bren guns. Immervoll was killed when Fw 190A-4/U8 Wk-Nr 145636 'Black 14' dived into the sea offshore from Cow Gap, at Beachy Head (*Andy Saunders Collection*)

A rare interception that prevented an attack took place on the morning of 5 February when four Focke-Wulfs of 10./JG 26 were met by a standing patrol of No 609 Sqn Typhoons as they attempted to raid Hailsham. The German pilots jettisoned their bombs and turned for home. One of the *Jabos* (Fw 190A-4 Wk-Nr 142435 'Black 1') lagged behind the other three, and after a chase it was shot down 30 miles south of Beachy Head by Flg Off Peter Nankivell. The pilot, Unteroffizier Herbert Büttner, was killed. Tragically, Flg Off Nankivell perished two days later.

On 26 February, 10./JG 2 raided Exmouth. In this case residential housing and a train were targeted, and a gas holder was repeatedly attacked with cannon and machine gun fire, causing it to burst into flames. But as the *Jabos* made their escape, Typhoons of No 266 Sqn intercepted. Sgt Richard Thompson's combat report stated;

'I was Yellow 2 on anti-Rhubarb patrol taking off from Exeter at 1200 hours. At about 1215 hours, Control called up and said Bandits were bombing Exmouth when we were off Dartmouth. We proceeded full throttle towards Exmouth until we were within about ten miles, when Yellow 1 [Sqn Ldr Charles Green] altered course to starboard until we were flying approximately southeast. We continued in this direction at full throttle, overtaking a Spitfire which had previously seen the e/a and [he] told us that the e/a were straight ahead. Shortly after passing the Spitfire, I saw four to six e/a flying very low over the water.

'Soon after, Yellow 1 opened fire and damaged one aircraft and then broke off and attacked another which I saw explode and hit the water. I followed the one that Yellow 1 had damaged which had one leg of its undercarriage hanging down. I opened fire at 200 yards and closed in to about 20 yards, but owing to my guns firing unevenly, I had great difficulty in keeping my aircraft steady. The e/a took mild evasive action and I closed in and pulled just over the top of it, probably very close to him because he hit the water at the same time and bits of his aircraft broke my spinner in half and did other minor damage. The broken spinner caused the engine to run very roughly, and I thought that I had engine trouble so I climbed steadily until we reached the coast. Landed at Exeter 1245 hours.'

The two *Jabos* shot down were flown by Unteroffizier Kurt Bressler (Fw 190A-5 Wk-Nr 152588) and Feldwebel Hermann Rohne (Fw 190A-4 Wk-Nr 735), both of whom were killed.

During February 1943, long-standing Channel Front regulars JG 26 had several *Staffeln* transferred briefly to the Eastern Front. They were temporarily replaced in northern France by elements of JG 54. For that reason 10./JG 26, which stayed behind on the Channel Front at Saint-Omer-Wizernes to continue 'hit and run' missions, was renumbered 10./JG 54 on 17 February.

A further loss for 10./JG 2 took place on 1 March when Unteroffizier Ernst Läpple, in Fw 190A-5 Wk-Nr 151106 'Blue 11', was shot down and killed. Approaching Bognor Regis, in West Sussex, at wave-top height, he was met by a standing patrol of two No 486 Sqn Typhoons. Läpple jettisoned his bomb and tried to run for home, the weapon's explosion throwing up a column of water which was ingested by the engine of one of the Typhoons, its pilot making a force landing near Sidlesham village. Flt Sgt Wallace Tyerman in the remaining Typhoon caught the *Jabo* and shot it down, his fighter's four 20 mm cannon again proving deadly.

Eastbourne was bombed once more on 7 March, but this afternoon attack was different from previous raids due to the increased number of *Jabos* involved, and the appearance of a different fighter-bomber unit on the Channel Front.

During December 1942 a new, dedicated *Jabo Geschwader* had been formed as *Schnellkampfgeschwader* (SKG) 10. Its commanding officer was Hauptmann Günther Tonne, who joined the *Jabo* ranks having previously undertaken Bf 110 *Zerstörer* operations with various heavy fighter *Geschwader*, including ZGs 1 and 76. He took up the post of *Kommodore* of SKG 10 on 1 January 1943, being promoted to Major at the start of the following month.

SKG 10's first actual operational constituent was III./SKG 10, created in North Africa by the renumbering of Oberleutnant Fritz Schröter's III./ZG 2. For northwest Europe combat, I. and II./SKG 10 were set up as paper entities during late 1942 but only activated in February 1943. Of these, I./SKG 10 took up residence at Saint-André-de-l'Eure, comparatively close to Évreux, under the command of Major Heinrich Brücker. He had seen combat in the Spanish Civil War with the *Legion Condor* and was an experienced Ju 87 Stuka pilot. Based at Caen-Carpiquet, II./SKG 10 was provisionally led by Oberleutnant Helmut Viedebantt. Also a former Bf 110 pilot with ZG 1, Viedebantt became II./SKG 10's permanent leader in May 1943, having been promoted to Hauptmann the previous month. From the start, these units were exclusively equipped with Fw 190s for *Jabo* operations.

The 7 March raid on Eastbourne included at least two II./SKG 10 pilots (including Leutnant Fritz Setzer and Major Walter Grommes), as well as airmen from the Channel Front *Jabo experten*, 10./JG 2 and 10./JG 26. The attack itself was another calamity for the British defences, with the 18-plus participating *Jabos* again reaching their target unopposed, resulting in 21 deaths, including seven military personnel.

SKG 10 next participated in a raid against Hastings on 11 March, which again caught the defences by surprise. This time, some 26 *Jabos* were involved, dropping most of their bombs on civilian areas in an afternoon attack that killed 38 people and injured 90. But this raid witnessed the first operational loss for SKG 10 when Fw 190A-5 Wk-Nr 150820 from 6. *Staffel*, flown by Feldwebel Kurt Barabass, was hit by light anti-aircraft fire. The badly damaged aircraft crashed into the sea just short of its temporary base at Coxyde, in Belgium, resulting in the pilot's death.

A further raid against London took place on the morning of 12 March, again launched from Coxyde, with 10./JG 2, II./SKG 10 and 10./JG 54 participating. Once more, the attack was covered by escorting Fw 190 fighters. The London areas of Barking and Ilford were targeted, resulting in 31 deaths and more than 40 injured. Yet again, the air raid sirens sounded too late.

The strike force was intercepted by Nos 122 and Norwegian-manned No 331 Sqns, but only after the attack had taken place. The latter unit, like No 122 Sqn, was equipped with the Spitfire IXs, which had entered service from June 1942 and had much improved performance over the earlier Mk VB. Based at RAF North Weald, No 331 Sqn shot down two of the *Jabos* – Feldwebel Emil Bösch of 10./JG 54 in Fw 190A-5 Wk-Nr

150829 'Black 12' and Oberfeldwebel Herbert Korth from 10./JG 2 in Fw 190A-5 Wk-Nr 157216. Both pilots were killed.

Two further *Jabos* were lost the following day. This time the target was Salcombe, in Devon, which was raided by at least five Focke-Wulfs of II./SKG 10. Fortunately, a standing anti-*Rhubarb* (looking for targets of opportunity) patrol of two No 266 Sqn Typhoons was in the area and vectored onto the fighter-bombers. In a textbook interception just after midday, Flg Off John Deall shot down one of the raiders, sharing the second victory with his wingman, Sgt David Eadie. Both 5./SKG 10 *Jabo* pilots were killed, Unteroffizier Erwin Ziegler in Fw 190A-4 Wk-Nr 147153 'White E' and Oberfeldwebel Hermann Schorn in 'White B' (sometimes called an A-5, but its visible Wk-Nr 2356 suggests it was actually A-4 Wk-Nr 142356).

The fighter-bombers returned to the Devon coast during the early evening of 23 March, and this time light anti-aircraft fire from the ground accounted for one of the *Jabos*. At least five Focke-Wulfs from II./SKG 10 attempted an attack in bad weather and were accurately targeted by the ground defences, the unit's *Gruppenadjutant*, Oberleutnant Oswald Laumann, being killed when his fighter-bomber was shot down near the Devon coastal village of Strete. He was flying Fw 190A-5 Wk-Nr 152544 'Green H', which also bore a black '*Schlacht*' triangle on its fuselage – several newly delivered Focke-Wulfs assigned to II./SKG 10 were finished at the factory with this marking, even though it was not appropriate for aircraft assigned to the *Jabo* mission.

The following day turned out to be another disaster for the defenders. A morning raid in numbers against Ashford, in Kent, was made by both 10./JG 2 and 10./JG 54. A railway town, Ashford was bombed several times during the war. On this particular occasion the Luftwaffe appear to have deliberately targeted its railway infrastructure and workshops, rather than resorting to an indiscriminate attack on civilians. Sadly, the bombing and strafing were accurate, with 51 civilians killed and more than 150 injured. This was to prove the deadliest day of the entire war for Ashford, with the locomotive works and a nearby motor garage being bombed. It resulted in considerable casualties and widespread destruction at both sites.

As it approached fast and low over the town, the Focke-Wulf of 10./JG 54's *Staffelkapitän*, Oberleutnant Paul Keller, was hit by light anti-aircraft fire. Still carrying its underfuselage bomb, the *Jabo* disintegrated in an enormous explosion. Keller was killed instantly, his aircraft (Fw 190A-5 Wk-Nr 152587 'Black 7') exploding directly overhead the Stanhay agricultural engineering works. It was destroyed in the blast, with at least 14 civilians killed. The only consolation for the town was the fact that two wardens sounded the 'Immediate Danger' warning (separate to the usual general air raid siren), which allowed many to rapidly leave their places of work to seek safety before Ashford was hit.

To add to the catastrophe, the subsequent interception of the fleeing survivors was a debacle, resulting in two No 91 Sqn Spitfire VBs being shot down by the raid's Fw 190 escort fighters from 5./JG 26, with one of the pilots being killed.

Oberleutnant Keller was replaced as 10./JG 54's *Staffelkapitän* by Leutnant Erwin Busch, with the unit's first mission under his leadership being a raid on Brighton close to midday on 29 March. This attack saw a return to indiscriminate bombing, resulting in 18 civilian deaths in various non-military locations across the Brighton area. As the *Jabos* fled the scene, they were intercepted by two Spitfire VBs of No 610 Sqn that just happened to be up on patrol from RAF Westhampnett, in West Sussex. Belgian pilot Flg Off François Venesoen fired at two of the Focke-Wulfs, causing them both to crash. One of the downed pilots was subsequently picked up by German air-sea rescue (ASR) personnel, but Unteroffizier Joachim Koch in Fw 190A-5/U8 Wk-Nr 152576 'Black 4' was killed.

The following day, II./SKG 10, now fully committed to Channel Front *Jabo* operations, raided targets in the Salcombe area, with three of the bombs falling on RAF Bolt Head airfield. Eight Focke-Wulfs were involved. Ventnor was attacked on 1 April by three *Jabos* from 10./JG 2, and just before midday on the 3rd a full-strength raid was carried out by both 10./JG 2 and 10./JG 54 against Eastbourne. Some 16 Focke-Wulfs were involved, resulting in 26 civilians being killed and 66 injured, as well as military casualties.

Once again, the *Jabos* got through uninterrupted, even though the method of attack was similar to previous missions against Eastbourne, with nearby Beachy Head being used as the local landmark from which to make the turn onto the target. Anti-aircraft defences did, however, fatally hit one of the raiders during the attack, Unteroffizier Fritz Ebert of 10./JG 54 abandoning his Fw 190A-5/U8 Wk-Nr 150835 'Black 11' over the Channel. He was never found.

10./JG 2 returned to Ventnor during the early morning of 7 April. Once again, the attack was not prevented, leading to considerable damage and the deaths of 16 civilians and injuries to more than 200 inhabitants. Ground fire resulted in the destruction of one of the raiders, Unteroffizier Günther Eschenhorn being killed while flying Fw 190A-5/U8 Wk-Nr 157209. As the surviving fighter-bombers fled, they were intercepted by Typhoons of No 486 Sqn. Two RAF Warmwell-based Typhoons from No 257 Sqn were also airborne, although the Isle of Wight was not their normal 'area of responsibility'. By chance, the Warmwell pilots happened upon the fleeing Germans, with Flg Off Peter Steib easily catching up with the Focke-Wulfs and despatching Fw 190A-5/U8 Wk-Nr 15258 flown by Unteroffizier Rudolf Radlewski, who was killed.

Folkestone was again targeted on 9 April, this time by four *Jabos* of 10./JG 54 in a late afternoon raid. Approaching from the northeast, upon reaching Beachy Head they turned inland and again dropped their bombs indiscriminately, killing three people and injuring 20 more. However, ground fire damaged Fw 190A-5/U8 Wk-Nr 150831 'Black 14', which subsequently crashed into the Channel. Its pilot, Unteroffizier Karl Heck, who had taken to his parachute, became the focus of a major ASR operation over which several aerial battles raged. Some of the covering aircraft were shot down by arriving RAF Spitfires and Typhoons, with no losses to the British fighters. Heck disappeared during the battle.

One of the units involved in his search was his own *Staffel*, 10./JG 54, with two of the *Jabos* being intercepted at around 1915 hrs by No 609 Sqn. Norwegian pilot Flt Lt Erik Haabjørn wrote in his combat report;

'I was flying as Red 1 with Sqn Ldr Lee as Red 2 in search of e/a patrolling ASR craft approximately ten miles off Gris Nez. We were flying for about

15 minutes up and down the Channel, unable to locate these, when we came across two FW 190s flying in fairly close formation approaching us head-on at 200 ft. I warned Red 2, and at the same time turned sharply after them. They broke away and we took one each.

'Mine twice tried to get away by going right down and keeping on a straight northeast course, which made it difficult for me to see him in the mist. Both times, out-of-range shots hitting the water all around him made him start weaving, and this enabled me to catch him up quicker. After four to five short deflection bursts, the 190 began taking heavy evasive action, but not really trying to out-turn me. He pulled straight up to 2,000–3,000 ft and turned on his back, where I got in a final burst at 250 yards. He jettisoned his hood and bailed out, the aircraft crashing 500 yards away from his parachute.'

The pilot, Leutnant Otto-August Backhaus, was killed. Flying Fw 190A-5 Wk-Nr 157290 'Black 12' at the time of his demise, Backhaus was the final combat loss suffered by 10./JG 54.

During April 1943, there was a significant change in the composition and designation of the *Jabo* units on the Channel Front. The two long-standing fighter-bomber *Staffeln*, 10./JG 2 and 10./JG 54 (the latter having originally been 10./JG 26), were amalgamated into a newly formed IV. *Gruppe* of SKG 10, becoming 13./SKG 10 and 14./SKG 10, respectively. The new IV. *Gruppe* was officially formed on 10 April at Cognac under Hauptmann Götz Baumann, with Major Heinz Schumann taking over from 13 May. Its *Stab*, 10., 11., 12. and 15. *Staffeln* were new units with no previous lineage.

Leadership of 13./SKG 10 was delegated to Leutnant Leopold Wenger, while Leutnant Erwin Busch continued his previous command of 10./JG 54 into its new form as 14./SKG 10. Leutnant Erhard Nippa, formerly of 10./JG 2, took over 15./SKG 10. The identification markings borne by the Focke-Wulfs of these *Staffeln* were also changed. The former numbering system carried on the fuselage sides of 10./JG 2, 10./JG 26 and 10./JG 54 aircraft was changed to a letter, the colour of which depended on the *Staffel* that the *Jabo* belonged to – although there is debate as to the colour of the letters borne by some of the aircraft.

There was also an influx of new pilots during April to fill the ranks of IV. *Gruppe*. SKG 10 had its own *Ergänzungsstaffel* advanced training unit, formed during November 1942, to give 'sharp end' instruction under operational conditions for new recruits.

SKG 10 was now the only dedicated *Jabo* organisation in the West, with more than 100 Fw 190s at its disposal. And April 1943 witnessed a brief alteration in tactics, with the introduction of two different mission profiles. One entailed the *Jabos* making attacks against USAAF heavy bombers, while the second involved missions against towns on the east coast of Britain, which temporarily bore the brunt of fighter-bomber attacks.

On 16 April 6./SKG 10 attempted to intercept an Eighth Air Force raid by B-17 Flying Fortresses of the 1st Bombardment Wing (BW), whose target was U-boat pens at Lorient. The eight Focke-Wulfs were intended to drop 250-kg bombs onto the American formation from above, the munitions exploding by means of proximity fuses. This unusual mission profile was tried out for a second time on 17 May by II./SKG 10, seven *Jabos* dropping 250-kg bombs from above on B-17s from the 1st and 4th BWs again attacking Lorient. No Flying Fortresses were reported lost due to the attempted interception, but the B-17 gunners appear to have shot down Feldwebel Karl Arndt, who was killed when his Fw 190A-5 Wk-Nr 151075 crashed at Saint-Avé.

The following day, *Stab./*SKG 10 Fw 190A-5 Wk-Nr 150892 and a twin-engined LeO 451 used by the unit as a liaison/transport aircraft were destroyed in an air raid on Poix airfield.

The first of the new attacks against east coast towns took place on the morning of 7 May with a raid by II./SKG 10 against Lowestoft, in Suffolk, and Great Yarmouth, in Norfolk. For this comparatively far-flung mission, the *Jabos* again utilised Coxyde. Once more, the *Jabos* achieved complete surprise thanks to their fast and low approach over water. Considerable damage was the end result, with the general air raid siren again coming too late. Although the defences made no clear response, Fw 190A-5 Wk-Nr 152526 'Yellow A' from 7./SKG 10 was lost with its pilot, Oberleutnant Willi Freudenreich, when the fighter-bomber hit a telegraph pole in Newport (in Norfolk).

A follow-up raid took place on the morning of 11 May, II./SKG 10 specifically targeting Great Yarmouth. Total surprise was yet again achieved, this time resulting in 49 killed, including a number of women from the Auxiliary Territorial Service. A unique interception followed as the *Jabos* fled the scene. Several Mustang Is of No 613 Sqn, using RAF Coltishall, in Norfolk, as a forward operating base, were on their way to an armed reconnaissance along the Dutch coastline. By accident, they happened upon the Focke-Wulfs, and a chase followed, with the Allison-engined fighters at the limit of their war emergency boost. The operational summary from No 613 Sqn's records noted;

'The initial dive of the leading Mustangs brought them to within about 400 yards of the Bandits, which were clearly identified by all the pilots as being 10 to 12 FW 190s flying in loose formation line abreast about 30 ft off the water. After two or three minutes chasing, Fg Off [John] Townsend, who was at 45 inches of boost and 2950 revs with an IAS of approximately 350 mph, closed to 250 yards and fired a three-second burst at the nearest e/a, which was more or less in the rear centre of the formation. Strikes were not observed but a cloud of black smoke streamed from the starboard side of the engine. Flg Off Townsend then closed and fired a slight deflection burst at the e/a, which was turning gently to port. More smoke followed. Finally, Flg Off Townsend closed to 100 yards and gave one more burst of about three seconds whilst closing to 25 yards. E/a then slowed up so quickly that Flg Off Townsend overshot. He pulled to starboard, and as he passed, the e/a hit the water and disintegrated.'

Leutnant Joachim-Peter Giermann of 5./SKG 10 failed to survive the downing of Fw 190A-5/U8 Wk-Nr 150822.

Undeterred by the loss of one of its pilots, II./SKG 10 returned the following day, escorted by the Bf 109Gs of II./JG 1, to target Lowestoft. This early morning attack by 13 *Jabos* was again successful in achieving complete surprise, the defences once more proving totally ineffective. One of the bombs dropped severed the Observer Corps' main emergency warning communications link, which was out of action when the next attack occurred. This took place just 24 hours later, and it was a raid in strength by around 24 *Jabos* from II./SKG 10.

Because radar had consistently proved to be ineffective in detecting the raiders due to their low and fast approach, the Observer Corps was a last line of defence in spotting in-coming fighter-bombers. However, with the communications out of action on the 13th, this new raid went completely undetected. In Lowestoft and the nearby village of Kessingland, 33 people were killed and more than 50 injured.

On 16 May another large-scale raid was mounted during the afternoon by several elements of SKG 10 against Lowestoft, but this time a barrage balloon concentration saved the day. Unfortunately, the *Jabos* instead attacked various other locations in Suffolk, including Felixstowe and Southwold, resulting in the deaths of ten civilians and leaving more than 24 injured. This time, the raiders ran into RAF Fighter Command in the form of Spitfire VBs from Polish-manned No 317 Sqn based at RAF Martlesham Heath, in Suffolk. Two of the fleeing Focke-Wulfs were hit hard, with Feldwebel Hans Burkhard of *Stab.*/SKG 10 being killed when Fw 190A-5 Wk-Nr 150892 crashed into the North Sea, while an Fw 190A-4 of 7./SKG 10 crashed on the Dutch mainland, its uninjured pilot eventually having been forced down almost certainly due to damage inflicted in the same action.

NOCTURNAL DEBUT

During this period a significant new role was added to SKG 10's *Jabo* activities with the introduction of nocturnal missions. This was to have far-reaching consequences for this *Geschwader*'s future operations, but the beginnings were a disaster. The Fw 190 was never intended for night flying in a combat environment, and the training of *Jabo* pilots at Cognac for this mission profile lagged behind. Few of the unit's airmen had previously

SKG 10 started flying nocturnal *Jabo* missions on the night of 16–17 April 1943. Completely lost, three pilots from the attack force landed by mistake at RAF West Malling. Fw 190A-4/U8 Wk-Nr 147155 of 7./SKG 10 was flown by Feldwebel Otto Bechtold, and his aircraft was parked directly in front of the watch office at the airfield. It was fitted with a large, streamlined Ju 87-type Weserflug-manufactured mounting beneath each wing for the carriage of a single 300-litre drop tank. The aircraft duly became the first intact *Jabo* to fall into British hands. *DO NOT TOUCH* warnings were rapidly scratched into the aircraft's temporary thick black finish (*Malcolm V Lowe Collection*)

undertaken night flying on a regular basis. Indeed, many of SKG 10's pilots were askance when orders were initially received for nocturnal raids, following a period of worrying rumours.

The first night *Jabo* mission against southeast England was undertaken on 16 April, flown principally by II./SKG 10 from Amiens-Glisy but with some pilots from I. *Gruppe* at Poix also involved. It did not go well. Two *Jabos* were lost in accidents even before nightfall, with one pilot being killed – during take-off for the raid itself, Oberleutnant Fritz Trenn of 3./SKG 10, an experienced former Ju 87 pilot from StG 77, collided with two other *Jabos* and perished in the resulting crash. At least one more Fw 190 was damaged before take-off, thus considerably reducing the strength of the attacking force.

During the mission itself, Feldwebel Werner Anrascheck was killed possibly as a result of anti-aircraft fire. Oberleutnant Hans Klahn, the *Staffelkapitän* of 2./SKG 10, died in a crash near RAF Staplehurst, in Kent, while several of the remaining pilots became hopelessly lost. Completely out of their depth, and wrongly assuming that RAF West Malling, in Kent, was an airfield on the French side of the Channel, three of the *Jabos* landed there, to the dismay of local RAF personnel.

Leutnant Fritz Setzer from 5./SKG 10, his aircraft damaged by anti-aircraft fire, made an exemplary emergency landing, only for his largely intact aircraft to be destroyed by the gunner in a Standard Beaverette airfield defence vehicle. It was probably the only time that the diminutive and very spartan Beaverette ever came into contact with the enemy. Oberfeldwebel Otto Schulz of 7./SKG 10 crashed short of the active runway and was injured. Completely lost, Feldwebel Otto Bechtold, also of 7./SKG 10, made a successful landing in Fw 190A-4 Wk-Nr 147155 'Yellow H' and was captured.

The first Fw 190 *Jabo* to fall intact and undamaged into British hands, the Focke-Wulf had warnings not to touch it hastily scribbled into the thick temporary black finish on the fuselage and underside of the engine cowling. The aircraft was subsequently flown to the Royal Aircraft Establishment (RAE) at Farnborough, in Hampshire, where it eventually received the British military serial number PE882 and was repainted in RAF camouflage and markings. After evaluation, the fighter-bomber flew with No 1426 (Enemy Aircraft) Flight until it was destroyed in a crash on 13 October 1944 that killed Flt Lt Ernest Lewendon, the Flight's CO.

Despite these losses, and the obvious inexperience of the German pilots in night flying, nocturnal missions for SKG 10 continued, with almost inevitable further problems. On 20 May 2./SKG 10's

After the capture of Feldwebel Otto Bechtold's Fw 190A-4/U8 at RAF West Malling, it was allocated the British military serial number PE882 and repainted in Dark Green/Dark Earth on its uppersurfaces contrasting with yellow undersides. Following its initial evaluation at RAE Farnborough, the fighter-bomber was passed on to No 1426 (Enemy Aircraft) Flight. The Focke-Wulf remained with the unit until it was destroyed in a crash that killed the Flight's CO, Flt Lt Ernest Lewendon, on 13 October 1944 (*Malcolm V Lowe Collection*)

Unteroffizier Heinz Ehrhardt landed at RAF Manston in Fw 190A-4/U8 Wk-Nr 145843 'Red 9', thus handing another airworthy Focke-Wulf to the British.

But for the time being SKG 10's main emphasis remained daylight 'hit and run' attacks on civilian targets. The brief foray into East Anglia during mid-May was followed by one of the most notorious and destructive raids of the whole 'hit and run' campaign. On Sunday, 23 May, a substantial simultaneous early afternoon mission was flown against Hastings and Bournemouth. At that time Bournemouth was a major reception centre for overseas military personnel on arrival in Britain. Whether or not this resulted in the centre of Bournemouth being targeted remains unverified to this day, but the result was deadly. Hastings was attacked by 20 *Jabos* from II./SKG 10, while 26 Focke-Wulfs from IV./SKG 10 raided Bournemouth.

The Hastings force flew as usual at wave-top height, and so went undetected until turning over land to head for the target. Bombs were dropped at 1256 hrs on several locations, demolishing a number of buildings including hotels on or near the seafront. Nearby Bexhill was also targeted. The result was 25 killed and around 80 injured. However, the Germans did not get away unscathed, with two *Jabos* being lost and their pilots killed as they attempted to flee back across the Channel. Oberfeldwebel Herbert Dobroch of 5./SKG 10, flying Fw 190A-4/U8 Wk-Nr 145834 'White L', was intercepted by the Typhoon of Flt Sgt W Ramsey from No 1 Sqn, based at RAF Lympne, in Kent, while Feldwebel Adam Fischer, in Fw 190A-4/U8 Wk-Nr 147156 'Black K', succumbed to anti-aircraft fire during the raid, his fighter-bomber crashing into the sea.

Four minutes after Hastings was targeted, IV./SKG 10 struck at Bournemouth. The attacking force made landfall east of Boscombe Pier near a prominent local natural landmark named Hengistbury Head shortly before 1300 hrs. A mixed formation of 26 Fw 190A-4/U8 and A-5/U8 *Jabos* appears to have made up the strike force – on 17 May 1943, SKG 10 reported a strength of no fewer than 109 available Focke-Wulfs of these marks.

The attacking force then wheeled inland to the west from its landfall and swept over the Boscombe area at almost exactly 1300 hrs, with some elements flying right across the centre of Bournemouth itself. Bombs rained down in an apparently haphazard fashion, with several of the Focke-Wulfs also taking the opportunity to strafe any apparently suitable targets that presented themselves.

The remains of Unteroffizier Friedrich-Karl Schmidt's Fw 190A-5/U8 of 15./SKG 10, which crashed into the St Ives Hotel on Grove Road after being hit by light anti-aircraft fire during the Bournemouth raid of 23 May 1943 (*Andy Saunders Collection*)

With the local anti-aircraft defences rapidly going into action, a considerable amount of small and medium anti-aircraft fire was quickly put up. One of the attackers crashed into 34 Grove Road just to the east of Bournemouth town centre, setting the St Ives Hotel on fire. The *Bournemouth Daily Echo* newspaper claimed the day after the raid that the Focke-Wulf (Fw 190A-5/U8 Wk-Nr 0136 'Yellow H') had been shot down by an RAF fighter. Its pilot, Unteroffizier Friedrich-Karl Schmidt of 15./SKG 10, was killed.

The Metropole Hotel at the Landsdowne in Bournemouth was partly destroyed during IV./SKG 10's raid on 23 May 1943. To this day, the exact death toll at the location is open to debate, with many RCAF personnel losing their lives there. Bournemouth was a major reception centre during that period for members of the RCAF arriving in Britain (*Malcolm V Lowe Collection*)

The bomb he was carrying did not explode until sometime after the crash – in the wreckage a diary was found stating that this was Schmidt's first operational mission. Also confirmed was the identity of his unit. He was probably shot down by light anti-aircraft fire from the roof of the East Cliff Court Hotel.

Across the Bournemouth area, the raid left a trail of destruction. In the town centre, the popular Beales department store had been completely wrecked and was on fire. Several other prominent local buildings had also been hit, in addition to many residential properties.

By far the worst single incident was in the Lansdowne area to the east of Bournemouth centre. Here, a well-known local landmark, the Metropole Hotel, received a direct hit. Opened almost exactly 50 years previously, this Victorian building was being used as a location for Royal Canadian Air Force (RCAF) airmen as a part of the local reception centre for Canadian personnel. A large number of Canadians, in addition to other nationalities, were just having their Sunday lunch as the raid commenced, and most of the military casualties on that day were at the Metropole. Also hit was the Central Hotel on Richmond Hill, where RAAF personnel were processed. Several were killed.

A group of IV./SKG 10 personnel in May 1943. Standing sixth from the left is Unteroffizier Friedrich-Karl Schmidt, while standing second from right is Unteroffizier Eugen Streich – both died on 23 May, the day of the attack on Bournemouth. Gefreiter Karl Laue, whose bomb killed 21 children during the 30 May raid on Torquay, is in the centre of the three kneeling pilots at right (*Andy Saunders Collection*)

The official death toll has been open to some debate in recent years, but it appears to have included at least 77 civilians (in addition to a civilian workman later killed in the subsequent demolition of the wreckage of Beales) and a large number of military personnel, with some 200 more injured. However, in her book *Incident 48 – Raid on a South Coast Town 1943*, local historian Angela Beleznay names just over 80 civilian casualties and quotes 131 military dead, with a further 89 unaccounted for. To date, these are regarded as the most accurate figures.

Mystery continues to circulate as to whether a second Focke-Wulf was shot down. Personnel of the 87th Light Anti-Aircraft Regiment, Royal Artillery stationed on the roof of Beales were certain that they had downed one of the *Jabos*, which several eyewitnesses stated crashed into the sea off Bournemouth Pier. It appears, however, that the damaged aircraft survived and returned to France. There, Unteroffizier Eugen Streich was killed when he hit a tree while flying Fw 190A-5/U8 Wk-Nr 840189. It has since been assumed that he participated in the raid, but there is also the possibility Streich was killed while performing a local training flight.

In the days that followed, SKG 10 carried out several more destructive raids. Just after midday on 25 May, 24 Focke-Wulfs of IV./SKG 10 targeted Brighton. Again, not intercepted before attacking, the *Jabos* dropped their bombs in several locations, leading to 24 deaths and 127 injured. While fleeing the scene, the aircraft were chased by Typhoons of No 486 Sqn, three of which were forward located at RAF Friston, near Brighton. The unit's commanding officer, Sqn Ldr Desmond Scott, attacked one of the *Jabos*, which hit the water and disintegrated. Unteroffizier Wilfried Braun of 14./SKG 10, flying Fw 190A-5 Wk-Nr 151377 'Black L', was killed.

In the opening weeks of May 1943, the formerly Spitfire VB-equipped No 91 Sqn received the superlative, and rare, Griffon-engined Spitfire XII.

Taken at Caen-Carpiquet, this photograph includes participants in the 23 May 1943 raid on Bournemouth. Third from the left is Leutnant Leopold Wenger of 13./SKG 10, whose aircraft is seen here parked at left with a small white '12' on its cowling. He had formerly flown this Fw 190A-5/U8 with 10./JG 2 as 'Blue 12'. Upon moving to 13./SKG 10 it was re-coded 'E', probably in white but possibly in blue (*Chris Goss Collection*)

The first of the production Griffon-powered Spitfires, this new type was optimised for low- to medium-level interception. Fast and well-armed (including a 20 mm Hispano cannon in each wing), it gave the hard-pressed RAF Fighter Command defences on the Channel Front a major new tool in the fight against the 'hit and run' Focke-Wulfs. Based at RAF Hawkinge, which was located just two-and-a-half miles north of Folkestone, No 91 Sqn was commanded by Sqn Ldr Raymond Harries.

During the evening of 25 May, II./SKG 10 targeted Folkestone with 19 *Jabos*. On this occasion the attack was thwarted, the Focke-Wulfs being detected by CHL radar in sufficient time to allow No 91 Sqn to scramble four of its new Griffon Spitfire XIIs. Led by Sqn Ldr Harries, who had just landed from an uneventful standing patrol and then immediately returned to the air, the Spitfires headed for nearby Folkestone. The sight of defending fighters for a change in the right place for an interception caused the *Jabo* pilots to jettison their bombs and run. During the ensuing chase, the Griffon Spitfires easily out-paced the Focke-Wulfs. In his subsequent combat report, Sqn Ldr Harries described the encounter as follows;

'I was leading Blue Section on a defensive patrol. I had just returned to base, and with my No 2, had just landed when the scramble signal was given from the watch office. We both immediately took off again, and saw enemy aircraft approaching Folkestone. I immediately dived towards the sea, the enemy aircraft turning back and jettisoning their bombs as soon as they saw us. Going over Folkestone, I experienced very heavy flak – fortunately inaccurate(!) – from our ground defences. I sighted one lone Fw 190 at sea level returning to France. I came in from his starboard side, delivering a three-second burst at 250 yards. The enemy aircraft hit the sea tail first, split in two and sank immediately.'

All four of the Spitfire pilots filed claims for shooting down more of the *Jabos* during the resulting combat, the initial stages of which were witnessed by many Folkestone inhabitants from the shore. In fact, only one Focke-Wulf was actually destroyed, although another returned to the Continent damaged with its wounded pilot. The aircraft shot down was Fw 190A-5/U8 Wk-Nr 152521 'Black M' flown by the *Staffelkapitän* of 6./SKG 10, Oberleutnant Josef Keller, who was killed.

Unfortunately, this success for the defences in preventing an attack was a rare triumph. On 30 May IV./SKG 10 undertook an afternoon raid with more than 20 Focke-Wulfs against Torquay that proved costly for both sides. Although detected, the Focke-Wulfs arrived unchallenged, with the general air raid siren only sounding after the attack had started. Underlining how low these raids were carried out, Fw 190A-5/U8 Wk-Nr 151365 struck the cross on a church spire and, out of control, crashed into a house and disintegrated. Its pilot, Gefreiter Karl Laue of 15./SKG 10, was killed. The bomb that the Focke-Wulf was carrying became detached and exploded when it hit the nearby St Marychurch, where children were attending

A portrait photograph of Unteroffizier Eugen Streich of IV./SKG 10, who was killed on 23 May 1943 in northern France. There has since been considerable speculation as to whether he died in a flying accident unconnected to the Bournemouth raid that day, or if he was the pilot of the damaged Fw 190 that some eye-witnesses in Bournemouth thought had crashed off Bournemouth Pier but had instead struggled back across the English Channel, only to crash in France (*Andy Saunders Collection*)

The crumpled remains of the BMW 801 engine from Gefreiter Karl Laue's Fw 190 A-5/U8 Wk-Nr 151365 of 15./SKG 10 is guarded in the Torquay road where the Focke-Wulf crashed on 30 May 1943. The bomb from this aircraft hit St Marychurch and exploded, killing 21 children attending Sunday School (*Andy Saunders Collection*)

Sunday School. The church was almost completely destroyed and 21 children killed.

In total, 45 civilians and five RAF personnel lost their lives and more than 150 civilians were injured, while destruction across the town was considerable. It was no consolation to the local inhabitants that this turned out to be the most costly raid for the Luftwaffe in the whole daylight 'hit and run' campaign. Two of the *Jabos* were shot down by light anti-aircraft fire and their pilots killed. They were Fw 190A-5/U8 Wk-Nr 840059 'Yellow D' of Unteroffizier Raimund Perlebach from 15./SKG 10 and Fw 190A-5/U8 Wk-Nr 840050 'Black A' flown by 14./SKG 10's Unteroffizier Erich Spät.

A third Focke-Wulf (Fw 190A-5/U8 Wk-Nr 151363 'Yellow F') also succumbed to the local defences, although its pilot was saved by an RAF ASR operation. Ditching some 18 miles off Berry Head, Unteroffizier Herbert Kanngeter of 15./SKG 10 was spotted by a Defiant pilot of No 276 Sqn and duly picked up by a Walrus.

A fifth *Jabo* was lost when Typhoons of No 247 Sqn from RAF Warmwell gave chase after the fleeing German fighter-bombers. The pursuit continued across the Channel until the Typhoon pilots caught one of the Focke-Wulfs as it flew over the island of Guernsey, at which point Flt Sgt Brian Calnan shot it down. The pilot involved is believed to have been Leutnant Hermann Müller in Fw 190A-5/U8 Wk-Nr 151412 'Blue F' of 13./SKG 10.

During the evening of the same day, II./SKG 10 mounted a raid on the East Anglian coastline against Walton-on-the-Naze and Frinton-on-Sea, both in Essex. Considerable damage was again caused as the attackers once more were unchallenged until they reached the two towns, with six civilians killed and 21 injured. It appears that the CHL radar site at Walton Tower was one of the intended targets. The raid was also costly for the Germans, with two *Jabos* being lost. Feldwebel Fritz Kessler of 5./SKG 10, flying Fw 190A-5/U8 Wk-Nr 150910 'White L', crashed into the water near Walton Pier and was killed – he had possibly lost control of his aircraft while avoiding one of his comrades. Leutnant Alois Harlos, his fighter-bomber (Fw 190A-5/U8 Wk-Nr 150824 'Yellow H' from 7./SKG 10) hit by light anti-aircraft fire, ditched at sea on his way home and was rescued by a Walrus, becoming a PoW.

June 1943 opened with further attacks, although it was to be a momentous month in a completely unexpected way. During the late morning of 1 June, 13./SKG 10 raided the Isle of Wight, with the St Catherine's Point lighthouse and the Niton radar installation (RAF Blackgang) being two of the targets specifically singled out in an apparently unusual attempt to strike multiple locations of direct military importance. Tragically, the attack on the lighthouse was accurate, its three Trinity House lighthouse keepers being killed.

In the early afternoon II./SKG 10 raided Margate, causing considerable damage there and in nearby Broadstairs, with ten civilians killed and various targets, including a gasometer, attacked. One of the participating

Focke-Wulfs, Fw 190A-5/U8 Wk-Nr 152529 'White R', was shot down and its pilot, Unteroffizier Otto Zügenrücker of 5./SKG 10, killed. His aircraft was either brought down by light anti-aircraft fire or by Typhoon pilot Flg Off Idwal Davies from No 609 Sqn.

The following early morning, II./SKG 10 raided Ipswich, in Suffolk, and nearby Felixstowe, escorted by II./JG 26. The majority of the strike force concentrated on the latter coastal target, although Ipswich had an important harbour and docks, albeit more inland. Three Focke-Wulfs attacked Felixstowe, but they were too low – Leutnant Hans Schate of 5./SKG 10 crashed and was killed, apparently hitting a crane in the docks area whilst at the controls of Fw 190A-5/U8 Wk-Nr 151375 'White B'.

On 4 June, Eastbourne was the target for IV./SKG 10 during the late morning. Once more, the attack by 18 *Jabos* was not prevented, although Spitfire XIIs of No 41 Sqn, flying from RAF Friston, intervened after the raid had taken place. Despite the best efforts of the town's anti-aircraft batteries, considerable damage was again caused, with seven civilians losing their lives and more than 30 injured. One of the pilots who participated in the raid, Leutnant Leopold Wenger of IV./SKG 10, noted the effectiveness of Eastbourne's gunners in his diary;

'Today we attacked Eastbourne with strong forces flying at low-level. We achieved considerable destruction. Certainly, the Flak fired considerably better than usual, and I was hit behind the engine by a 2 cm shell which went through the whole aircraft. Several instruments failed and a small splinter went into my leg. I had more than enough trouble bringing my "kite" home in one piece.'

Although 'Poldi' Wenger returned to France despite his aircraft being damaged, a direct hit from a newly arrived Scottish light anti-aircraft gun

The afternoon raid of 30 May by IV./SKG 10 on Torquay resulted in many civilian casualties. It was also the most costly raid for the *Jabos* in the whole 'hit and run' campaign, with five Focke-Wulfs lost. This was the wreckage of Gefreiter Karl Laue's Fw 190A-5/U8 Wk-Nr 151365 of 15./SKG 10 that crashed into houses on Teignmouth Road, the explosion of its bomb killing 21 children in their nearby Sunday School class (*Andy Saunders Collection*)

During the morning attack against Eastbourne on 4 June 1943, the *Gruppenadjutant* of IV./SKG 10, Oberleutnant Kurt Hevler, was shot down and killed when his Fw 190A-5/U8 Wk-Nr 151353 – marked with his rank chevron – ended up on its back after the pilot attempted a forced landing on marshland behind the Star Inn at Normans Bay. Its demise was another success for locally based light anti-aircraft gunners (*Andy Saunders Collection*)

The name 'Metropole' was often used for south coast hotels in the 1930s, and like its equivalent in Bournemouth, Eastbourne's Metropole Hotel was hit and partly demolished when the town was targeted yet again in early June 1943, just before the daylight 'hit and run' *Jabo* campaign came to an abrupt end (*Andy Saunders Collection*)

crew brought another of the Fw 190s down a few miles east of Eastbourne. Chevron-marked Fw 190A-5/U8 Wk-Nr 151353 ended up on its back when Oberleutnant Kurt Hevler (*Gruppenadjutant* of IV./SKG 10) attempted a forced landing on marshland behind the Star Inn at Normans Bay. The pilot was killed in the resulting crash.

Eastbourne was again attacked two days later in the early afternoon of 6 June, the town being targeted on this occasion by II./SKG 10. Once more, the raid was not intercepted before its arrival, and the subsequent bombing left five civilians and five military personnel dead, with 24 civilians and five servicemen injured. Leutnant Helmut Wenk was at the controls of one of the attacking Focke-Wulfs, and he subsequently recalled;

'As we neared the target, we shifted from our cruising formation, line abreast by *Schwarme*, into our attack formation, line astern. At the same time we opened up to full power, flying about 10 m above the sea to avoid British radar. Just before we crossed the coast, the leader pulled up to about 300 m and we followed, turning in to attack. Plunging down through the Flak, we released our bombs in a *Steckrubenwurf* [turnip-lob] shallow dive attack, then got back to low level and curved round to port to escape round Beachy Head and out to sea.'

As the *Jabos* fled, they were pursued by several Spitfire XIIs of No 91 Sqn. In the subsequent chase, one of the Focke-Wulfs was caught and shot down by the combined efforts of Plt Off Dennis Davy and Sgt John Watterson. The downed aircraft, Fw 190A-5/U8 Wk-Nr 151376 'Yellow G', was flown by Leutnant Dominikus Miller of 7./SKG 10, who was killed.

And then there was nothing. In a totally unexpected bolt from the blue, the daylight 'hit and run' campaign against the south of England came to an abrupt end. Events far from the Channel Front intervened to cause the rapid withdrawal of most of SKG 10's assets to southern Europe, where the Allies were threatening to invade Sicily, having wrapped up the conflict in North Africa during mid-May 1943. Both II. and IV./SKG 10 moved from the Channel Front to Italy, joining III./SKG 10 already in-theatre. Only I./SKG 10 was left in France, and this *Gruppe* was by then committed to nocturnal *Jabo* operations against southern England with the Fw 190.

Subsequently, only occasional daylight strafing attacks were carried out by regular Focke-Wulf-equipped fighter units, these aircraft never being armed with bombs. By the autumn of 1943, due to the much reduced threat of daylight 'hit and run' bombing raids, standing patrols of Typhoons had been replaced by pairs of Hawker fighters parked at readiness at their assigned coastal airfields.

For the rest of 1943 and into 1944, I./SKG 10 continued its nocturnal fighter-bomber activities against coastal towns, shipping and, occasionally, military installations in the south of England, but rarely in the large numbers that had characterised daylight *Jabo* operations earlier in 1943. During these sorties, the Focke-Wulfs were intercepted by RAF Mosquito nightfighters using their on-board radar to detect incoming raiders in a way that had not been available to the defenders earlier in the war throughout the 'hit and run' daylight campaign. On 20 June 1943 another pristine nocturnal arrival at RAF Manston was Fw 190A-5/U8 Wk-Nr 152596 'White 6' flown by Unteroffizier Werner Öhne of 1./SKG 10. The aircraft subsequently became PN999 and was flown by No 1426 (Enemy Aircraft) Flight until it was eventually scrapped.

Losses continued. For example, on 26 November 1943 3./SKG 10's Unteroffizier Bogdahn Faul was shot down and killed by anti-aircraft fire in Fw 190G-3 Wk-Nr 160419 'PP+SO'. Nevertheless, by late that year, I./SKG 10 had become very proficient in night operations, the Fw 190 having been virtually re-born and reinvented as a nocturnal attack aircraft.

This capability was put to use by the Luftwaffe when a new bombing campaign was initiated against the British Isles. Operation *Steinbock* was intended as a night bombing offensive, and its participants were mainly twin-engined medium bombers, but also included the larger Heinkel He 177 and the Fw 190A-5 *Jabos* of I./SKG 10. *Steinbock* was nicknamed the 'baby blitz' by the British, but it was anything but small in size, and included several very damaging raids on British towns and cities that resulted in more than 1500 deaths. The role of I./SKG 10 was to complement the operations of the bigger bombers with their much greater payload, while continuing its own *Jabo* operations.

The renewed targeting by the Luftwaffe's larger and longer-range bombers started with operations in the weeks prior to *Steinbock*. This began badly for I./SKG 10 when, on the night of 2–3 January 1944, the unit lost four Focke-Wulfs, one being shot down by a Mosquito nightfighter of No 96 Sqn. On the eve of *Steinbock* (20 January), I/.SKG 10 reported 25 Fw 190s of various marks on strength, with 20 operational. The *Gruppe*'s headquarters had been located at Rosières-en-Santerre, east-southeast of Amiens, since October 1943, but it used forward locations such as Caen-Carpiquet when necessary.

Steinbock commenced on the night of 21–22 January with an attack on London. Over the following weeks the campaign ran into many logistical and operational problems that severely affected the capabilities of the Luftwaffe bombers. Compared to the strategic bombing campaign being mounted nightly during that period by RAF Bomber Command against German cities and towns, *Steinbock*'s stuttering attacks were seemingly piecemeal. The whole operation finally ground to a halt in late May.

Alongside the *Steinbock* missions, I./SKG 10 had continued with its *Jabo* attacks, often against south coast ports that were increasingly suspected to be preparing for the anticipated Allied invasion of France. On 23 May I./SKG 10 mounted a raid on Portsmouth, losing Fw 190G-8 Wk-Nr 190092 'Yellow 3' of Feldwebel Otto Heinrich, who was killed. Exactly two weeks later, the whole course of the war dramatically changed.

CHAPTER FOUR

D-DAY AND AFTER

With prominent flame dampers on individual exhaust stacks, these Fw 190G-2s fitted with Messerschmitt underwing carriers for drop tanks were photographed during the invasion period in June–July 1944. The aircraft almost certainly belonged to I./SKG 10, which continued, when possible, to mount nocturnal as well as daylight operations against the Allied invasion forces *(Malcolm V Lowe Collection)*

There is a long-held fallacy, encouraged by the 1962 motion picture *The Longest Day*, that the Luftwaffe did very little to counter the D-Day landings on 6 June 1944. This basically incorrect 'fact' is now so entrenched in popular folklore that it has become necessary for historians ever since to put the record straight. The reality is that the Luftwaffe *did* attempt to do what it could to counter the Allied landings on D-Day, in the face of the massive aerial presence on that chaotic day and in the weeks that followed. This led to a considerable amount of aerial combat, involving not just the units locally based in France and the Low Countries, but increasingly including *Gruppen* that were rapidly relocated to the Channel Front in response to the Allied landings.

In early June 1944, the Luftwaffe's fighter forces in the west were as thin on the ground as they had been in the preceding three or so years. The large-scale reduction of Luftwaffe units on the Channel Front following the lack of overall success in the Battle of Britain, and the relocation of most frontline *Geschwader* to the east for involvement in the invasion of the Soviet Union, had left just a small core of *Gruppen* in the West which were familiar foes to the Allies. Thus, the Luftwaffe's fighter order of battle in France and the Low Countries on 6 June 1944 comprised elements of the highly experienced JGs 2 and 26 under *Luftflotte* 3. Also present was the erstwhile foe of Britain's home defences since it was formed, I./SKG 10.

In mid-1944, the overall strength of SKG 10 was still depleted since a significant part of this *Geschwader* had been rushed to the Mediterranean 12 months earlier. It had left just I./SKG 10 available for operations on the Channel Front. Similarly, the *Steinbock* campaign had taken its toll on operability. Nevertheless, this *Gruppe* still presented a considerable menace to Allied operations, especially due to its cadre of experienced pilots and the unit's night-flying capabilities. Indeed, during the spring of 1944, the *Gruppe* had acted with some success as a makeshift nightfighter unit, countering increasing Allied nocturnal activity over the Channel Front as the possibility of invasion drew ever closer.

In early June, I./SKG 10 was led by Hauptmann Kurt Dahlmann. Having used the airfields of Roye-Amy and Rosières-en-Santerre during the first half of 1944, the *Gruppe* was anticipating a possible invasion somewhere along the Normandy coastline. Dahlmann's *Gruppe*, plus elements of III./SKG 10, moved in early June to Évreux-Fauville airfield in preparation for the invasion that was becoming widely expected amongst Luftwaffe personnel. By then the unit had operated Fw 190G *Jabo-Rei* long-range fighter-bombers for several months, these aircraft supplementing the ranks of its existing Fw 190A *Jabos*. At that time the unit reported 33 Focke-Wulfs on strength, but of these only 19 were serviceable.

During the late evening of 5 June, I./SKG 10 flew a *Jabo* mission against Portsmouth, and it was as these aircraft were returning in the early hours of the 6th that Dahlmann began receiving the alarming news from Generalfeldmarschall Hugo Sperrle's *Luftflotte* 3 headquarters in Paris that gliders had been reported landing in the vicinity of Saint-Lô, and that other Allied activity, including parachute drops, was also taking place. Dahlmann ordered an armed reconnaissance to take off with all due speed to check these reports. Among the pilots who participated was Oberfähnrich Wolfgang Zebrowski of 2./SKG 10, who had just returned from the raid on Portsmouth and now had a new assignment. He later wrote in his book '*Nachts über den Wolken*' ('*Night Flight above the Clouds*');

'We received the order to rapidly make ready all available aircraft to intercept the infantry-carrying gliders and their towing aircraft that had been spotted over Saint-Lô. Visibility was poor when we took off, the night being very dark. Arriving in the specified area, I looked out for flashes of light that would signal machine gun fire while constantly zig-zagging – but there was no sign whatsoever of gliders! By then running low on fuel, I headed back to *Évreux*. We were disappointed by our lack of success; none of us had seen the enemy.'

But the *Gruppe*'s luck was about to change. Dahlmann duly received a new alert, stating that British bombers were operating in the area between Carentan and Caen. He ordered Hauptmann Helmut Eberspächer, the *Staffelkapitän* of 3./SKG 10, aloft to verify the information, and to look for the gliders and parachutists that Zebrowski's reconnaissance had failed to discover.

One of the pilots in the vanguard of the chaotic and ferocious fighting over Normandy was Hauptmann Kurt Dahlmann, CO of I./SKG 10. He received a Knight's Cross for his leadership of the *Gruppe* on 6 June and in the days immediately following the invasion (*Tony Holmes Collection*)

A graduate of the fighter-bomber training unit KG 101, Eberspächer had originally been assigned to 3./SKG 10 during the late spring of 1943 and had been promoted to Hauptmann in May 1944. His small force in the early hours of 6 June comprised four Fw 190 *Jabos*, which took off in the darkness from a small field near the Loire river and headed north. On arriving at the coast, he subsequently reported;

'Little by little, the horizon began to light up, and each passing moment brought confirmation of what was happening down below. It was a massive spectacle. More and more, the silhouettes continued to emerge off the coast of hundreds of ships. Directly in front of, and parallel to, the coastline were American warships firing at the German emplacements of the Atlantic Wall. Landing craft were making their way towards the beaches. The invasion that we had long waited for had begun.'

Running short of fuel, Eberspächer and his contingent of *Jabos* was about to turn for home when he caught sight above them of the RAF heavy bombers that he had been sent to find. He continued;

'My aircraft was only carrying enough fuel for two hours in the air, and it was approaching the time to consider heading back to our home airfield. But just as I made the decision to return home, I spotted above me a formation of British bombers.'

The German pilots had indeed discovered the RAF aircraft. But the British crews were unaware that they had been located by a potentially deadly enemy. Due to the cloudy conditions, the Lancasters had descended to a bombing altitude lower than they would have normally used. This gave Eberspächer and his fellow pilots an opportunity that they immediately exploited. In the ensuing interception, Eberspächer shot down three Lancasters, while one of his pilots, Feldwebel Kurt Eisele, also claimed a four-engined bomber. The Lancasters were part of a large strike force that included Nos 50, 97, 106, 463 and 467 Sqns, whose primary target was the coastal battery at Saint-Pierre-du-Mont.

Eberspächer's victims fell in the vicinity of Isigny-sur-Mer and Carentan between approximately 0501–0506 hrs that morning. They have subsequently been identified as Lancaster IIIs ND739/Z and ND815/G of No 97 Sqn from RAF Coningsby, in Lincolnshire, and Lancaster III ND874/R of No 50 Sqn from RAF Skellingthorpe, also in Lincolnshire. But Eisele's victory has been the subject of some conjecture in recent years. Originally thought to have also been a Lancaster, it now appears more likely that it was English Electric-built Halifax III MZ513/K of No 578 Sqn, part of a force that was attempting to bomb the coastal battery at Mont Fleury.

Thus it was that SKG 10's *Jabos* had been the Luftwaffe's first response to the Allied invasion on 6 June, ironically standing in as makeshift nightfighters. Eberspächer and his three fellow pilots were jubilant upon their return to base, but also fully aware that the invasion had started, and that many much more difficult battles lay ahead. The commencement of the invasion of Occupied Europe, codenamed Operations *Neptune* and *Overlord*, on 6 June would mark a very sinister turning point for the Luftwaffe in the West, and begin a decline that would gather pace in the months to come.

At Lille-Nord airfield, the *Geschwaderkommodore* of JG 26, the celebrated fighter pilot Oberstleutnant Josef 'Pips' Priller, had also been made aware by *Luftflotte* 3 headquarters during the pre-dawn hours of 6 June that the invasion

On the morning of 6 June 1944, the *Geschwaderkommodore* of JG 26, Oberstleutnant Josef 'Pips' Priller, and his wingman, Unteroffizer Heinz Wodarczyk of 4./JG 26, made their famous low-level, fast-firing pass along a small part of the D-Day invasion beaches, which has since been completely erroneously called the Luftwaffe's only response to the Allied landings on that day. Priller (at right with flowers) was photographed later that month receiving congratulations on his 100th aerial victory (a B-24 downed west of Dreux on 15 June). Unteroffizer Wodarczyk was killed in action during Operation *Bodenplatte* on 1 January 1945 (*EN Archive*)

had started. Elements of his *Geschwader* were scattered around France, with a major move of personnel and aircraft already underway that was completely separate to the unfolding events in Normandy. Indeed, some elements of JG 26 were actually being relocated – on orders from higher authority – *away from* northern France. Stationed at Priller's Lille-Nord headquarters was the *Stab* and 4./JG 26, with 1./JG 26 at Lille-Vendeville and 2. and 3./JG 26 at Denain, southwest of Valenciennes. They were therefore nearest to the invasion area, but had been ordered to move south to Reims.

II. *Gruppe* of JG 26 was in the south of France at Biarritz and Mont-de-Marsan, while part of III. *Gruppe* was already moving south. News of the invasion caused an immediate change of plans, with I. and III. *Gruppen* ordered to Creil, north of Paris, and to Cormeilles-en-Vexin, northwest of Paris, while II. *Gruppe* very quickly began moving from the south of France northwards, with several of the unit's Focke-Wulfs leaving Biarritz at 0700 hrs. Some of the Fw 190s carried a passenger in the cramped confines of the fuselage behind the cockpit, it being possible with the relocation of internal equipment to squeeze a suitably sized groundcrewman through the radio hatch in the port fuselage side.

Priller later wrote of his frustration concerning plans to move part of JG 26 away from northern France, where this elite and battle-hardened fighter wing would potentially be most needed when the invasion began;

'On the 6th of June, the II. *Gruppe* of my *Geschwader* was on R&R [rest and recuperation] at Mont-de-Marsan, I. *Gruppe* was in the process of transferring to Reims and III. *Gruppe* with their Me 109s was on the way to Metz. These changes were ordered by II. *Jagdkorps* [which JG 26 was subordinated to under *Luftflotte* 3]. Eight days before the order for these movements, I had a spat with the commander of this higher command, Generalmajor [Werner] Junck. I warned him of the imminent invasion, and pointed out to him that in the circumstances these transfers were unjustifiable. Generalmajor Junck replied that, as a fighter wing commander, I was in no position to make judgement on the development of the [higher command's] overall grand strategy!'

With Priller's administration work achieved as far as he was able to locate and send northwards the various elements of his unit, he and his wingman, Unteroffizer Heinz Wodarczyk of 4./JG 26, took off from Lille-Nord at 0800 hrs on the 6th for an armed reconnaissance of the unfolding situation to the west along the Normandy coastline. By that time the Allied landings were in full swing, the initial assault wave having been intended to go ashore at 0630 hrs. Interviewed after the war, Priller explained, 'I told Heinz to stay close, but in any case he knew to do this. We did not know what we would find'.

The pair flew west at low altitude on what was to become one of the most famous flights of the entire war. Dodging into cloud cover when possible to avoid Allied fighters, the two lone Focke-Wulfs emerged from the gloom in the vicinity of the British/Canadian *Sword* Beach. With Wodarczyk faithfully following his leader, the two Focke-Wulfs swooped down along the coastline to around 50 ft, with all machine guns and cannon firing. Taken by surprise, the Allied anti-aircraft gunners put up an immediate barrage, but the German flyers made a fast and clean escape. Exercising extreme care on the way home to avoid the many Allied fighters and fighter-bombers by then operating over Normandy, Priller and Wodarczyk safely reached Creil airfield.

During subsequent years this single mission has been portrayed as the Luftwaffe's only attempt to attack the Allied invasion forces on 6 June, but in reality a variety of other units flew many sorties that day. These little-known and rarely publicised operations were separate, but additional, to the many actual fighter missions mounted by the Luftwaffe aimed at countering the swarms of Allied aircraft operating over the invasion area and further inland. At airfields across northern France, Luftwaffe aircraft from Fw 190s and Bf 109s to Ju 88s and other frontline types became embroiled in one of the most hectic days of aerial warfare in the whole of World War 2.

Such was Allied aerial supremacy during the D-Day period that any Luftwaffe aircraft in northern France had to be carefully and thoroughly hidden when on the ground to avoid immediate air attack. Fw 190G-3 'White 9' of I./SKG 10 was photographed in its improvised 'hide', with 300-litre drop tanks beneath its wings. Most, if not all, Luftwaffe personnel in northern France prior to D-Day had expected the Allied invasion to come, many anticipating the event with trepidation (*Hans Meier Collection*)

The airfields used by the Luftwaffe aircraft were targets for the numerous Allied fighter-bombers operating over Normandy and beyond, and in many cases the German warplanes had to be concealed amongst trees or other cover to prevent them from being spotted and attacked while still on the ground.

In the thick of the aerial battle from the earliest moments was I./SKG 10. Following the initial interception of RAF Bomber Command aircraft in the early hours of 6 June, the unit began flying missions against the invasion fleet later that morning. One of the pilots involved was Oberfähnrich Wolfgang Zebrowski of 2./SKG 10, who had searched in vain for signs of the initial Allied activity during the early hours following his return from raiding Portsmouth. Taking off from Évreux at approximately 1100 hrs, he was part of a four-aircraft *Schwarm*. Zebrowski later wrote;

'We were flying at an altitude of 1500 m. As we approached Le Havre, coming out of cloud cover, I suddenly found myself alone. My three comrades had disappeared. My radio calls remained unanswered, so I continued alone, altering my course to approach from the southwest the armada of Allied ships described by the colleagues who had intervened on the beaches before me. The sky was full of enemy fighters flying both above and below the clouds. They probably thought it was impossible for a German to be mad enough to come and venture into this area.

'After crossing the coast, the enemy ships were soon in sight. All at once I saw, aligned from north to south, and protecting the eastern flank of the invasion fleet, three battleships or heavy cruisers. A few destroyers reinforced their flanks. Majestic, the ships were there in front of me and their spectacle fascinated me. The idea then came to me to try to sink one of them.

'It was surely utopian, if not downright presumptuous, to think of reaching them and using my two machine guns, two cannon and a 500-kg bomb. But why not try and, if luck smiled on me, I might be awarded the Knight's Cross? The risk was really great – these ships opposed me with their defences of quadruple anti-aircraft guns, and I had nothing on my side but the element of surprise: no one could imagine that a German aviator would risk himself in these parts to attack a combat ship. I dived through the cumulus clouds towards the ships from an altitude of 2000 m

The Fw 190G had entered operational service approximately a year prior to D-Day, flying nocturnal operations with I./SKG 10 on the Channel Front against southern England. Its ability to carry underwing 300-litre drop tanks considerably increased the aircraft's range, allowing some aircraft of I./SKG 10 to be based outside the immediate and most dangerous area of operations following the invasion. Nevertheless, with the Allies enjoying aerial supremacy over Normandy, the unit's operational capabilities were severely limited (*Malcolm V Lowe Collection*)

On D-Day itself and in the weeks that followed, I./SKG 10 was heavily involved in the air war over northern France, attempting to bomb Allied invasion shipping as well as ground forces as they advanced inland. These three G-series *Jabos* (an Fw 190G-2 is nearest with underwing Messerschmitt carriers) were probably photographed at Dreux, I./SKG 10 flying many sorties from this airfield (*EN Archive*)

until I found myself on their left beam. Then I banked onto the left wing and attacked in a dive, the ship well centred in my gunsight, firing with all my machine guns and cannon.

'My shells and bullets hit the deck of the ship. I could see their impacts thanks to the luminous trails of the tracers. The surprise seemed total, the crews were trying above all to take cover, without firing at me. At 600 m, I corrected my trajectory to drop my bomb. I felt a shock, while anti-aircraft shells exploded around me. I thought that was the end of me. But, as if by a miracle, I got away with only a small wound to the nose, due to shrapnel, which I only became aware of when drops of blood fell on my flight suit. At low altitude, I flew over the sea towards the mainland, glancing back in the hope of perhaps seeing the ship sink, but it was already too far behind me and I was too low. With my last drops of fuel, I returned to Évreux.'

Several conventional fighter units, willingly or otherwise, soon became involved in air-to-ground sorties on 6 June. One of these was 3./JG 2, whose pilots were transformed into makeshift *Jabos* during the hurried and sometimes chaotic Luftwaffe response on D-Day itself. In similar fashion to JG 26, JG 2 was also in the process of being scattered as June 1944 dawned. The wing's I. *Gruppe* was stationed at Cormeilles-en-Vexin, but in the days before 6 June the *Gruppe*'s *Staffeln* had been moved to several landing grounds in the vicinity of Nancy. II. *Gruppe* was in Germany, at Gütersloh, being reconstituted, having suffered substantial losses on the Channel Front. III. *Gruppe* was moving to Fontenay-le-Comte in Normandy. News of the invasion quickly changed the *Geschwader*'s plans, and like JG 26, elements of the wing were soon moving so as to be stationed nearer to the invasion beaches.

Amongst the pilots of 3./JG 2 was Leutnant Wolfgang Fischer, and the morning of 6 June turned out to be very eventful for his *Staffel*. Awoken at 0500 hrs with news of the invasion, Fischer and his fellow airmen of the unit departed Nancy to fly to Creil one hour later. On arrival, they were informed that their Fw 190A fighters were going to be transformed into stand-in fighter-bombers with the installation of W.Gr.21 rocket tubes beneath their wings.

This weapon had already been used for several months by other units against USAAF heavy bomber formations, with variable amounts of success, but the W.Gr.21 was, in theory, equally applicable for air-to-ground work. Its success, however, depended on employment by pilots trained in its usage. Fischer and his fellow pilots had no experience whatsoever with this weapon. In addition, only one of the heavy, unguided rockets could be carried under each wing, thus requiring a good shot with this limited armament array in order to have any positive effect. The large, externally mounted rocket tube beneath each wing also created drag and affected the flying characteristics of the Fw 190 for those unfamiliar with the W.Gr.21.

The Focke-Wulfs configured to fire these rockets against USAAF heavy bombers over Germany were equipped with a special control panel in the cockpit. Such a modification was absent from the aircraft of 3./JG 2, with Fischer being informed instead that the firing button for his rockets would be the red release button beneath his instrument panel normally used to drop the centreline external fuel tank. Electricians had hastily re-wired this release button for its use with the underwing rockets, while the pilots of 3./JG 2 were given rudimentary instruction as to how to aim the weapon.

With only the standard *Revi* 16B gunsight mounted in their Focke-Wulfs, Fischer and his fellow pilots had little to go on for accurate aiming. Worse, they were informed that the rockets had a tendency to fly off to the right when fired, so it was necessary to aim to the left when releasing them to compensate for their rather unusual trajectory. Not surprisingly, the airmen were not at all impressed with their rapid conversion into *Jabo* pilots.

During the wait for the armourers to re-wire his Focke-Wulf, Fischer tried to calculate how he would attack an Allied ship using his gunsight. All too soon, it was time for his first experience of being a *Jabo* pilot. In his post-war memoirs, he described the subsequent mission;

'We took off at about 0930 hrs. We were flying in three *Schwarms* – 12 aircraft, 24 rockets in all. Major [Erich] Hohagen [the *Gruppenkommandeur* of I./JG 2] was not part of this mission, and so Hauptmann Josef Wurmheller [*Staffelkapitän* of 9./JG 2] led the formation in his place.

'With a rocket under each wing, we couldn't carry our usual belly [fuel] tank. But in any case we didn't need it. The Focke-Wulf had a range of 900 km and the round trip to the target area was only half that distance. Our objective was the landing beaches northeast of Bayeux (which I later learned were code-named *Gold*, the most westerly of the three British invasion sectors). The cloud cover was seven-tenths. The conditions were ideal for what we had to do. The large congregation of Allied fighters – Spitfires, Mustangs, Thunderbolts and others, which could be seen patrolling the clear sky in gaps between the clouds – had less chance of falling on our formation, which was crossing the cumulus clouds one after the other to hide from their eyes.

'Half-an-hour later, we passed in the vicinity of Bayeux, where I could see that the fighting was already raging. In order to deceive the enemy,

Leutnant Wolfgang Fischer (right) of 3./JG 2 made a W.GR.21 rocket attack on an Allied cargo ship off the invasion beaches on the morning of 6 June. The following day he was shot down attempting to make a repeat attack on shipping near Bayeux (*Tony Holmes Collection*)

An ordnance NCO (note the crossed rifles on his lower left sleeve) from I./JG 2 leans nonchalantly against a heavily armed Fw 190A-6 in mid-June 1944. To his right is a loaded W.GR.21 tube housing a 21 cm projectile (*Tony Holmes Collection*)

we continued straight over the Bay of the Seine for several minutes, having planned to launch our attack when we arrived from the sea. From our altitude of 3000 m, I had a panoramic view of the entire invasion zone, which extended from the mouth of the Orne River and from Caen in the east to the Cotentin Peninsula in the west. A veritable armada, in the purest sense of the word, was spread out before my eyes. Having not experienced any of the previous landings in the Mediterranean, I had no way of appreciating the importance of this new attempt by the enemy. Even if I was not totally impressed by this spectacle, its scale gave rise to the first serious doubts in my mind. Would we really be able to repel such a powerful force?

'Undisturbed by fighters or marine Flak, we completed our run-up towards the open sea over the bay, then turned back towards the largest concentration of troop transports. Because of the cover of enemy fighters over the beachheads, we had neither the time nor the opportunity to position ourselves for a broadside attack.

'We were to stick to a high-speed pass towards the shore (the same direction, of course, that most of the ships were pointing), with an attack from behind causing us to pass very low over them and prevent proper aiming [by the ships' gunners]. But as we approached, I saw that the ship directly in front of me was, in fact, across my path, exposing its flank. With growing excitement, I shifted my aeroplane so that I had three-quarters of the ship's length to the left of my sights and prepared to fire my rockets.

'It was only when I was really close to the boat, when the target became very big, that I realised, seeing a small white plume that was emanating from its bow, that the boat was not at a standstill at all, but that it was in fact moving slowly to the left and that it was also turning. I immediately reduced my speed so as not to exceed the firing distance of 1000 m and I turned very slightly to the left as well, realigning my aim a good length ahead of the ship. When I estimated that it had become big enough to occupy the entire diameter of my gunsight (if I had kept it entirely in the viewfinder), I pressed the red button. For a second, I was enveloped by a ball of brilliant flames, and the sound of a thousand howling devils assailed my ears.

'Having never fired a rocket before in my life, I was seized with panic. I didn't know what to expect, but certainly not something this terrifying. The other pilots were also firing their rockets, and for a moment it was as if the sky around me was filled with fiery comets. Although the rockets did not cause recoil when fired, my aeroplane gave a slight lurch as it was released from the combined weight of the two missiles. I then quickly pointed the nose of my aeroplane down to the ground and rushed towards the shore. Crossing the beach at an altitude of 300 m, I fired my guns at the masses of men and equipment piled up below me. After the spectacular and noisy fireworks that had accompanied the departure of the two rockets, the hammering of my two cannons, drowned in the roar of my engine, sounded like the harmless cracking of a cap pistol.'

As intended, following his adventure, Fischer landed at Chamant, near Senlis, just before 1100 hrs on an improvised landing strip in the grounds of a small mansion. He later learned from a fellow pilot who had witnessed his attack on the transport vessel (probably a Liberty cargo ship) that one of his W.Gr.21 rockets had struck the ship and exploded, with the other weapon narrowly missing the stern.

The *Staffel*'s Fw 190s were rearmed and refuelled whilst hidden from Allied aircraft under convenient trees bordering the small landing ground. Fischer expected to be flying again on the next mission, but instead was stood down. Along with some fellow airmen, he spent the afternoon of D-Day relaxing at the municipal baths in Senlis.

For the Luftwaffe pilots who were charged with attacking the invasion beaches on 6 June and subsequent days, the sight of the huge armada of ships, and the substantial numbers of Allied troops on the ground, was an awe-inspiring and worrying sight. As for Leutnant Wolfgang Fischer, the war would not last much longer. The following day he was shot down by anti-aircraft fire in his Fw 190A-6 while making a repeat attack on shipping near Bayeux. He spent the rest of the war as a PoW.

The remaining pilots of JG 2 were kept busy flying both fighter-bomber sorties against the invasion fleet and more routine air-to-air sweeps in their attempt to counter Allied aircraft supporting *Overlord*.

It was not just JG 2 that used the W.Gr.21 in the air-to-ground role during the D-Day period. Another unit that employed this ordnance was I./JG 26, which had several of its Fw 190A fighters fitted with a single-shot drag-producing launch tube beneath each wing. This improvised *Jabo* arrangement was not well-liked by the *Gruppe*'s airmen, and the ad hoc armament was best suited to the *Revi* 16D gunsight, which, according to some pilots, was apparently not fitted to all of I./JG 26's Focke-Wulfs.

Nevertheless, from around 15 July some of the unit's aircraft were converted to employ the W.Gr.21 for use principally against Allied armour, which by then was inland from the invasion beaches. Indeed, by that time, the original landing areas were of less importance, the fight having moved on into the interior of Normandy and beyond. Elements of I./JG 26 were flying from Cormeilles-en-Vexin and Boissy-le-Bois when this requirement was added to the unit's operational capability, with the *Gruppe* for a time being referred to as the *Jagdgeschwader*'s *Werfergruppe* (rocket[-firing] group).

Its first mission was flown on 16 July, but the operation was aborted due to bad weather. The following day, I./JG 26's rocket-equipped Fw 190s ran into Allied fighters, but on the 19th conditions were more favourable and an attack was made against British armour in the Caen area. A similar mission was flown on 20 July, although thereafter bad weather again intervened.

Boissy-le-Bois was little more than a landing strip southwest of the town of Beauvais and to the north of the airfield at Cormeilles. Usefully, it had partly wooded surroundings which allowed I./JG 26's Focke-Wulfs to be parked amongst the trees for cover from marauding Allied fighter-bombers. Its grass landing strip was camouflaged so as to suggest a trench system to further mislead any hostile airmen overflying the area. These were the desperate lengths that the Germans were having to go to during the D-Day period to try and conceal their precious aircraft and personnel, such was the aerial domination of the Allies.

DEADLY ENCOUNTERS

Also present in France during mid-1944 was the only dedicated *Schlacht* unit at that time based in the west, *Schlachtgeschwader* (SG) 4. Its III. *Gruppe* had been formed during October 1943 when there was a major reshaping of Luftwaffe attack units, its immediate ancestor being the Fw 190-operating III./SKG 10. This *Gruppe* was already in southern Europe in mid-1943 when its removal south to join other elements of SKG 10 was partly responsible for the major scaling down of the *Schnellkampfgeschwader*'s 'hit and run' campaign against southern England at that time.

Led by Major Fritz Schröter, III./SKG 10 had subsequently been heavily involved in the bitter fighting on Sicily in July 1943 due to the Allies' successful invasion (Operation *Husky*), and then over mainland Italy following the Allied landings during September 1943 (Operations *Avalanche*, *Baytown* and *Slapstick*). During this campaign it had operated virtually alongside both I. and II. *Gruppe* of SG 4, which were long-established in the aerial battle over southern Europe.

As a result of the ensuing armistice in Italy in September 1943, the country had effectively been split into two, with the south supporting the Allies and the north continuing to fight on alongside Germany. This rapidly developing situation had necessitated a repositioning and reorganisation of locally based Luftwaffe units. III./SKG 10 duly moved from Guidonia and Furbara, both in the vicinity of Rome, to Graz, in Austria, where the *Gruppe* was reconstituted as III./SG 4 on 10 October 1943. This was a part of the major restructuring of the air-to-ground assets of the Luftwaffe taking place at that time, in which the *Schlacht* arm was considerably expanded and reorganised. The new commander of III./SG 4 was Major Werner Dedekind, although he was replaced within weeks by Major Gerhard Weyert, who was a *Legion Condor* Ju 87 veteran. He had also flown the Stuka during the early months of World War 2 with 11./LG 1.

Graz was simply an initial location to allow for the new *Gruppe* to be established away from the frontlines, and so in November 1943 the unit moved to Beaumont-sur-Oise, in northeastern France. A further temporary relocation was made the following month to Laon-Athies, before the *Gruppe* settled into its longer-term home from February 1944 onwards of Clastres, to the northeast of Paris. Its pilots eventually flew a mixed-bag of Fw 190s, including A-6s and A-7s, in addition to some *Schlacht* and *Jabo*-configured Focke-Wulfs. Like I./SKG 10, III./SG 4 came under the overall organisational direction of *Luftflotte* 3.

A brief deployment was made by elements of III./SG 4 from Clastres to Le Luc near Toulon, in southern France, for anti-submarine operations, which proved to be fruitless and a waste of valuable resources. In early June, 8./SG 4 was posted to Le Luc to continue this unproductive task. Within days, all three *Staffeln* and the *Stab* of III./SG 4 were overtaken by events. At the start of June the *Gruppe* reported 40 Focke-Wulfs on strength, of which a creditable 36 were serviceable.

Like other commanders of Luftwaffe units, Major Weyert was alerted to the news of invasion early on the morning of 6 June. According to the unit's war diary, he was contacted at 0300 hrs by Major Heinrich Fahrenberg, the *Derfflinger Ia* at *Generalstab der Luftwaffe* (operations officer at the Luftwaffe headquarters), who told him the disquieting news that airborne forces had landed to the north of Caen, and a seaborne invasion had commenced (although at that time no beach landings had been made by the Allies, and Fahrenberg had apparently been wrongly briefed that the amphibious assault was near the mouth of the River Seine).

With a re-arrangement of internal equipment it was possible to carry a passenger (usually from the groundcrew, although in this view a photographer) in the rear fuselage of the Fw 190. This was dangerous at the best of times, as the additional aircrew could not wear a parachute. The transfer flights conducted on 6 June 1944 particularly by SG 4 resulted in the deaths of several such passengers when the aircraft they were travelling in were shot down (*Malcolm V Lowe Collection*)

At 0645 hrs, with a lack of further information, Major Weyert ordered III./SG 4 to the highest state of readiness. An hour later, he received orders from *Derfflinger Ia* to prepare a move to forward airfields, but there was a crucial delay in the issuing of the actual order to deploy, which did not come until 0935 hrs. This caused a hold-up that was to prove costly.

Nevertheless, preparations were soon underway to deploy SG 4's assets to strike at the invasion beaches, which were by then known to be on the Normandy coastline near to and to the west of Caen. This involved rapid transfer flights to suitable airfields in the proximity of the invasion area. At that time, *Stab* and 9./SG 4 were stationed at Clastres (a small landing ground at Frières, near Clastres, was also used), 8./SG 4 had been ready to settle into the pleasant surroundings of Le Luc, in the south of France, and 7./SG 4 apparently had aircraft at both Clastres and Le Luc.

The airfield at Laval was chosen for the *Stab*, 7. and 9. *Staffeln*, while Tours was the planned destination for 8./SG 4. With the *Gruppe* split between northeastern France and the south, some of the unit's assets had a long journey to reach Laval and Tours airfields. In order to facilitate the rapid preparation of the Focke-Wulfs upon arrival, most aircraft would carry a groundcrewman in the fuselage for their rapid deployments. This proved to be a highly dangerous undertaking.

Several transfer flights comprising multiple Focke-Wulfs for mutual protection were made by SG 4 on 6 June, but a number of these were intercepted by Allied fighters, with disastrous consequences for some of the German personnel. The first transfer flight of seven Fw 190s took place during the morning, the pilots with their groundcrew passengers following railway tracks as a useful navigation aid.

On the 6th, many aerial combats took place between Luftwaffe and Allied aircraft. Piecing together which particular pilots and units were involved in each individual combat is often difficult due to the huge amount of aerial fighting that occurred. However, with some certainty, it is possible to place a number of pilots in a particular location at a particular time to explain the participants of at least some of the combats that took place, although historians tend to disagree rather than concur on this subject.

One of the most successful units of the Eighth Air Force's VIII Fighter Command was the 56th Fighter Group (FG) based at RAF Boxted, in Essex, which flew the P-47 Thunderbolt throughout its time in combat over northwest Europe. The group's 62nd Fighter Squadron (FS) was engaged in its own fighter-bomber work on 6 June over northern France, while also looking out for any signs of Luftwaffe aerial activity. The big, radial-engined Thunderbolt possessed plenty of power for this type of operation, and had the advantage of water-injection to increase the engine's output for short periods during combat.

While strafing a locomotive near Rambouillet at around 1050 hrs, 1Lt William McElhare of the 62nd FS chanced upon the SG 4 transfer flight. The American pilot, together with other flyers from his unit, did not hesitate to engage the German aircraft. McElhare's combat report stated;

'I saw an Fw 190 at 500 ft coming down the tracks from the east at 8 or 9 o'clock to me. He evidently saw me and started to turn. So I poured the coal on it and we swung into a Lufbery. As we climbed, circling, I used water, managing to keep above the Hun. Continuing to tighten the circle, I was gradually catching up on him and forcing him lower and lower. Just as I was about to draw deflection and fire, he reversed his turn, snapped violently, and dived into the deck from about 300 ft. The enemy aircraft exploded in a huge mass of flame and smoke.'

The German fighter was Fw 190A-7 Wk-Nr 430472, flown by the *Gruppenadjutant* of III./SG 4, Oberleutnant Johann Pühringer. He was carrying an Unteroffizier groundcrewman as his passenger, and both men were killed when the Focke-Wulf struck the ground near Brétigny. An experienced former fighter pilot who had also served as an instructor, 29-year-old Pühringer was the type of seasoned flyer that the Luftwaffe could ill afford to lose.

In the same combat, another pilot from *Stab* III./SG 4, Unteroffizier Max Rahofer, had a lucky escape. Flying Fw 190A-6 Wk-Nr 650502, his aircraft was damaged, but he managed to flee unscathed. His Obergefreiter groundcrew passenger was wounded, however.

A further transfer flight of III./SG 4 attempted to head towards the invasion area during the afternoon of 6 June, but it too was discovered by American fighters. This time it was the Thunderbolts of the Eighth Air Force's 78th FG, operating from RAF Duxford, in Cambridgeshire, and led by the unit's CO, Lt Col Frederic C Gray Jr. The USAAF pilots were seeking locomotives and rail facilities in the vicinity of the southern Normandy town of Alençon when they chanced upon the Fw 190s. Immediately giving chase, both Gray and 1Lt Vincent Massa of the group's

83rd FS fired at the 'tail-end Charlie' Focke-Wulf, Fw 190A-6 Wk-Nr 470601 'Black M'.

Gray later explained in his official 'Account of Combat';

'I led 78th Group to Alencon area with the mission of destruction of lines of communication. Arrived over area 12,000ft and stooged around a couple of holes in the overcast. My wingman sighted a train and I sent him down for it, following on his wing since I had not seen it. We broke out at about 3,000ft and dropped our bombs at the train, with poor results, getting only near misses and a few on the track. We then strafed it and allowed it to blow off steam. I then took my flight up the line to Alencon and out each rail line from the city for perhaps 20 miles without sighting any rail traffic other than two locos in the M/Y [marshalling yard] at Alencon, which I passed up due to the presence of many civilians in the immediate area who were waving at us.

'At this time my Red Leader sounded off on a gaggle of FW 190s on the deck moving south near the city. I finally saw them and tagged on, passing him [the Red Leader] and coming up on tail-end Charlie. I was catching him without water until he threw his souped-up charge in when I had to hit mine. I caught him easily and he started turning. All those boys I taught back at Matagorda would have got a kick out of my sorry deflection shooting. I finally got him going straight and got four pretty good bursts into him. He jettisoned his canopy as his engine cut out and started [to climb] out. I was about to overshoot him, and skidded out to the side, when Lt. Massa gave him a burst. He overshot him and eased up alongside and watched him laboriously crawl out, his jacket and helmet on fire. He got out about 600ft and his chute worked beautifully.'

The Focke-Wulf's pilot, Hauptmann Heinz Mihlan, bailed out before the aircraft crashed at Saint-Jean-d'Assé, northwest of Le Mans in the modern-day Sarthe department of the Pays de la Loire. His passenger, Feldwebel Hans Eidam, was killed. Gray and Massa were each credited with a shared half-kill for this action.

At roughly the same time (1540 hrs), a second Focke-Wulf (Fw 190A-6 Wk-Nr 470582 'Black B') was shot down in the vicinity of Le Mans by the 83rd FS. It too belonged to 8./SG 4. The victorious American pilot was 1Lt Peter Caulfield, who explained in his combat report;

'Cargo White Flight bounced a section of five to eight Fw 190s flying south on the deck just west of Mayenne. The enemy aircraft were being pursued by two planes of Cargo Red Flight. The e/a made a 90 degree right turn into us. I fired several short bursts at the e/a, already being engaged by other P-47s. I then singled one out and began firing at him in a turning circle. After hitting him heavily, the e/a dished out, rolled, spun, and then crashed.'

Lt Col Gray added, referring to the time immediately after his own victory;

'I then broke for another [Fw 190], but just as I was about to try my deflection shooting again my 2nd element leader, Lt. Caulfield, beat him up. He turned into me and snapped into the ground, making one hell of a beautiful explosion which I caught in my camera – only now they tell me the damned thing jammed.'

The Focke-Wulf that 1Lt Caulfield shot down was flown by Feldwebel Franz Brauneis, with Unteroffizier Paul Ebert as the passenger. Both were killed when the aircraft crashed at La Bazoge, some seven miles to the north of Le Mans.

The destination of some of the SG 4 transfer flights – Laval airfield in the department of Mayenne in modern-day Pays de la Loire – was, in theory, sufficiently away from the invasion area to avoid too much Allied air activity. In reality, however, this was certainly not the case. Laval attracted attention as soon as SG 4 started arriving at, and flying from, the airfield.

One of the USAAF units operating in the Laval area during the afternoon of 6 June was the Ninth Air Force's 15th Tactical Reconnaissance Squadron (TRS), stationed at RAF Middle Wallop, in Hampshire. It was equipped with the North American F-6C, a camera-carrying version of the P-51B/C Mustang. Although a reconnaissance platform, the F-6C was nevertheless fully armed, and USAAF reconnaissance pilots were just as adept at aerial combat as their fighter pilot brethren.

An early evening incoming transfer flight of 7./SG 4 with Laval airfield as its destination proved to be a complete disaster. Flying in the vicinity of the airfield were Mustangs of the 15th TRS, who caught several of the Focke-Wulfs as they were nearing Laval. Fw 190A-6 Wk-Nr 650303 'White A' flown by Oberfeldwebel Martin Kolberg was shot down five miles southeast of the airfield, both the pilot and his passenger, Obergefreiter Erwin Ohlwein, being killed. In the same combat, Fw 190A-6 Wk-Nr 470585 'White L' of Unteroffizier Otto Speer was also destroyed in the vicinity of Laval, with the pilot losing his life. On this occasion Speer's aircraft appears to have not been carrying a passenger.

These two losses were almost certainly the Fw 190s claimed at Laval by 2Lt Ernest Schonard and 1Lt Clyde East of the 15th TRS. Schonard also claimed a second Focke-Wulf damaged. For East, this was his first confirmed victory, and he subsequently went on to be the highest-scoring reconnaissance pilot in the Ninth Air Force.

Several other members of the transfer flight that Schonard and East intercepted at Laval had lucky escapes. Unteroffizier Karl-Heinz Schängel wisely returned to Clastres, while Unteroffizier Gerhard Jäckel diverted to Haute-Fontaine and Unteroffizier Adolf Görtz found temporary sanctuary at Angers.

Despite these losses, III./SG 4 was nevertheless able to mount three missions from Laval during the late afternoon and evening of 6 June against targets both offshore and inland at Lion-sur-Mer, Ouistreham and Saint-Aubin-sur-Mer. Ouistreham is the port for Caen, lying on the coast just north of the strategically vital city, with Lion-sur-Mer a short distance to the west of Ouistreham, these being important objectives for the Allies on D-Day and immediately after.

The first of these forays saw a *Schwarm* of four Fw 190 *Jabos* of III./SG 4 take off from Laval at 1719 hrs, led by the *Staffelkapitän* of 9./SG 4, Oberleutnant Heinrich Hesse. Their objective was Allied shipping off Saint-Aubin-sur-Mer. The four Focke-Wulfs reached their target area and each dropped a 500-kg bomb, claiming hits on two landing craft, despite a curtain of anti-aircraft fire. Using the overcast skies for cover, the quartet of Fw 190s successfully returned to Laval at 1810 hrs.

This was a very wise choice of target, for Saint-Aubin-sur-Mer was a vital objective for Canadian forces at the eastern end of *Juno* Beach on 6 June. The small raiding force of Fw 190 *Jabos* was sent to aid the German defenders at that location who had been under attack in a specially prepared strongpoint designated WN 27 (part of the German 'Atlantic Wall'). The Canadian troops were assisted by the amphibious Duplex Drive Sherman tanks of C Squadron, 10th Canadian Armoured Division (The Fort Garry Horse). The landing ships offshore that the Fw 190 *Jabos* attacked had been providing bombardment fire for the Canadian soldiers. But the token III./SG 4 force could do little to affect the outcome of the fight, which was effectively over by the evening of 6 June in that area.

Just as Hesse's Fw 190s landed back at Laval, the Mustangs of the 15th TRS arrived and shot down the incoming transit flight Fw 190s of Kolberg and Speer, disrupting preparations for further III./SG 4 operations until later that evening. The second raid by the unit, therefore, was another small-scale assault, this time led by Leutnant Karl-Ludwig Klepke. According to the SG 4 war diary, the four-aircraft *Schwarm* bombed Allied forces in and around what has since been immortalised as 'Pegasus Bridge' in the sector south of Ouistreham. Each aircraft carried a 500-kg bomb, and they dropped them at 2007 hrs before again making a very rapid escape. One of the Focke-Wulfs was damaged by anti-aircraft fire but survived.

The last of the three missions flown by III./SG 4 on D-Day was mounted from Laval at 2100 hrs. It was a five-aircraft raid led by Oberleutnant Hesse, who had commanded the initial attack from Laval several hours earlier. The pilots of the four Fw 190 *Jabos* led by Leutnant Klepke in the previous mission had observed the enormous number of Allied ships offshore near Ouistreham and Lion-sur-Mer, and these were now the objective of Hesse's small Fw 190 *Jabo* force. But the mission was rapidly aborted in the face of intense anti-aircraft fire and the presence of Allied fighters – that time of evening is still light over Normandy in early June. The *Jabo* pilots instead attacked any targets that were less heavily defended, of which there were very few, before diverting to Angers in the growing darkness and landing at 2215 hrs.

In the hours and days following the Allied landings along the Normandy coast on 6 June, many Luftwaffe Fw 190 and Bf 109 fighter units were rushed to the area as an attempted counter to the massive aerial presence covering the invasion, and to act as impromptu *Jabos* to attack land and sea targets. Amongst the Focke-Wulf *Gruppen* and *Staffeln* involved was 11.(*Sturm*)/JG 3 with its Fw 190A-8/R2 fighters normally employed on anti-bomber operations. One of the unit's pilots was Unteroffizier Willi Maximowitz, seen here taxiing in following a sortie in the invasion area (*Malcolm V Lowe Collection*)

The diarist of SG 4, in concluding the disastrous day's activities, noted the four pilots of III./SG 4 killed and the deaths of the four groundcrew passengers, concluding that to carry such additional personnel should be discontinued. The anonymous writer also noted that the order from higher authority to deploy onwards to Laval and Tours from Clastres and Le Luc should have been given much sooner during the early hours of 6 June.

At 0430 hrs in the early morning of 7 June, two Junkers Ju 52/3m trimotor transports departed from Clastres carrying unit personnel, including groundcrewmen. They should have done so during the afternoon of 6 June, but the increasingly chaotic situation for the Germans on D-Day, and the danger of Allied fighters, meant that such deployments now needed to be made at night. Indeed, it was not until 9 June that a full servicing team was able to reach Laval to work on III./SG 4's *Jabos* with the correct know-how to support the operations of a fully fledged Fw 190 *Gruppe*. Their appearance was welcomed at the airfield by the few unit personnel who had deployed there on 6 June.

Laval had proven to be totally unprepared for the arrival of III./SG 4's Fw 190s on D-Day, the base having only having been returned to operational status during the winter of 1943–44. The diarist of SG 4 complained in the *Schlachtgeschwader* official history that the airfield lacked refuelling trucks and bomb-loading equipment, and there were no local personnel to assist in turning around the arriving *Jabos* in readiness for operations. Additionally, there was little or no airfield defence in the form of Flak batteries. Safe dispersals were also at a premium. The harassed base commander at Laval had been incorrectly told that elements of SG 4 would not arrive until the evening of 6 June, and that they would not fly any operations until the following day.

From approximately 0600 hrs on 7 June, four missions were mounted by III./SG 4 from Laval comprising some 23 aircraft against British and Commonwealth troops and armour in the mouth of the River Orne. But three of these operations met strong fighter opposition and were driven away, with the *Jabo* pilots dropping their bombs randomly. The first of these, comprising five Focke-Wulfs, was caught by Allied fighters north of Caen and forced to abort.

Adding to III./SG 4's woes, the Allies were now well aware that Laval housed a potentially dangerous adversary. At around 1000 hrs on 7 June, the airfield was attacked by USAAF fighters, which shot up the base and destroyed four Fw 190s and at least two of the equally vital Ju 52/3m transports. Leutnant Günther Esau of 7./SG 4 was shot down in aerial combat south of Laval in his Fw 190A-6 'White F', the pilot bailing out injured. That evening, at about 2100 hrs, two Fw 190 *Jabos* of 8./SG 4 were intercepted by USAAF fighters and shot down as they attempted to reach Laval. Oberleutnant Walter Dahlem was wounded when his Fw 190A-6 'Black D' crashed.

Operations continued for III./SG 4 on 8 June. According to the unit's war diary, three missions comprising 17 Fw 190 *Jabos* were mounted from 1240 hrs, the targets including troops going ashore at Riva Bella and a bridge over the River Orne at Benouville. The first of these operations was led by III./SG 4's commander, Major Weyert, and included eight *Jabos*, but it was aborted due to the presence of Allied fighters. The Fw 190 pilots had to jettison their bombs while making a timely escape.

The second mission, again led by Weyert, comprised five *Jabos* and included a much-needed escort provided by the Fw 190A fighters of I./JG 11, led by the *Staffelkapitän* of 3./JG 11, Oberleutnant Hans Schrangl. I./JG 11 was one of the many Luftwaffe fighter *Gruppen* that had been rushed to the invasion area at that time, the unit's normal home being Bonn-Hangelar in Germany. For its temporary assignment in France, I./JG 11 was stationed at Rennes-Saint-Jacques from 7–20 June. Achieving a rendezvous between different units for specific missions was difficult due to take-off times being compromised by the considerable Allied air activity over the Luftwaffe's airfields.

8 June also saw Feldwebel Willi George of 9./SG 4 shot down and posted as missing. That evening, Major Weyert attended an emergency conference at the headquarters of *Fliegerführer West*, which was responsible for the control of ground-attack units following the Allied invasion of France. Very little was achieved to redress the rapidly deteriorating situation for the Luftwaffe in the invasion area, it being obvious that local air superiority was now firmly in the hands of the Allies.

Further attempts were made on 9 June to fly operations from Laval, but only an evening attack on the Allied landings at Riva Bella could be made. Then, during the night of 9–10 June, disaster struck. A raid by heavy bombers on Laval caused significant damage, the main runway being rendered inoperable due to several direct hits. It was impossible for III./SG 4 to generate sorties as a result of the bomb damage, so the *Gruppe* was released from operations on 10–11 June.

Following repairs to the runway and infrastructure at Laval, missions resumed on the 12th, by which time the Allies were making significant headway on the ground and piecemeal fighter-bomber operations by the Luftwaffe were likely to achieve little. Nevertheless, at 0635 hrs, a four-aircraft *Schwarm* took off for a further strike on Allied forces at Riva Bella. This mission failed because of the presence of enemy fighters, with all pilots having to jettison their bombs. According to the unit's diary, later that day four Fw 190 *Jabos* were destroyed on the ground by yet another attack on the airfield.

In the days and weeks following D-Day, *Oberkommando der Luftwaffe* (Luftwaffe High Command) relocated as many *Jagdgruppen* as it could spare to northern France to help the beleaguered Luftwaffe units already operating there. This included several *Gruppen* that were sorely needed for anti-bomber operations over Germany, but which were now equally required to help combat the Allied forces in the air as well as on the ground in Normandy. With the Allies increasingly gaining a foothold in France following the invasion, many Luftwaffe fighter pilots found themselves having to fly air-to-ground sorties.

Dreux was also used by elements of I./SKG 10 during that time. As soon as it became obvious to the Allies that this airfield was important to the Luftwaffe in the German response to the invasion, it was attacked. On both 10 and 13 June, the USAAF bombed the airfield and its related infrastructure, inflicting considerable damage.

Hauptmann Kurt Dahlmann was awarded the Knight's Cross of the Iron Cross on 11 June 1944 in recognition of the performance of his *Gruppe*

An Fw 190G-3 or G-8 of I./SKG 10 (thought to be 'Brown 6' of 2. *Staffel*) with an unusual munition beneath the fuselage that appears to be an AB 250 anti-personnel bomblet-releasing container. It was probably photographed at Évreux-Fauville airfield, which was much used by SKG 10 during the D-Day period (*EN Archive*)

over Normandy on and after D-Day. Eventually, I./SKG 10 moved to Tours, and it continued operations from the airfields in the vicinity of that important town on the Loire river for several more weeks.

Finally, with the airfields at both Laval and Tours under attack by Allied aircraft, the operations of III./SG 4 were increasingly limited as the time passed following D-Day. And then came a complete change of emphasis for the *Gruppe*. In the centre of France, a major uprising of French partisans had commenced in the weeks leading up to D-Day, which in reality tragically turned out to be premature. Air and ground forces were rushed to the area by the Germans in order to quell this significant rebellion, which included the use of gliderborne forces and an influx of Luftwaffe assets. Although still sorely needed in Normandy, III./SG 4 was one of the units that was sent to the area.

To that end, on 19 June, virtually the whole remaining airworthy complement of the unit's Fw 190 *Jabos*, including several newly delivered examples, began to leave the invasion area. They were flown to Clermont-Ferrand airfield, in today's Auvergne-Rhône-Alpes region of south-central France. Some aircraft were prevented from making the trip due to the continuing bad weather in Normandy. The next day, Major Weyert flew from Villacoublay, near Paris, to Bourges to meet with Oberst Hermann-Josef Freiherr von dem Bongart, who was the leader of the recently created anti-partisan unit *Geschwader Bongart*.

One of the less well-known Luftwaffe combat units of the later war period, this *Geschwader* was formed in mid-April 1944. At once III./SG 4 became the most potent component of the new wing, and duly flew a number of missions in support of German anti-partisan operations. However, on 30 June, the *Gruppe* received orders to transfer to the Eastern Front, beginning straight away on 1 July. It duly came under the control of *Luftflotte* 1 for operations on the northern sector of the front, moving to Jacobstadt in modern-day Latvia.

However, III./SG 4 was not the only Fw 190 *Jabo* unit to fly in central France during that period. A little-known *Staffel* that operated Focke-Wulfs in the fighter-bomber role was 10./ZG 1, which was based in central France during 1944. It began life in July 1937 as a maritime patrol unit, later being designated 5./*Bordfliegergruppe* 196 and equipped with Arado Ar 196 floatplane fighters at Brest/Süd, in Brittany, from where it flew operations over the Bay of Biscay.

From March 1943, its capabilities were significantly enhanced with the arrival of Fw 190s that were to be flown alongside the Ar 196s. Two months later the *Staffel* became 1./*Seeaufklärungsgruppe* (SAGr) 128. This reflected its increased capability and expanded role, the drop tank-equipped Fw 190A-5s being able to patrol in the vast expanse of ocean southwest of Cornwall and out to the Isles of Scilly in an effort to protect French-based

U-boats heading to and returning from the Atlantic. However, the mission profile of this unit was to be radically changed due to the deteriorating war situation for the Germans.

In January 1944, 1./SAGr 128 was re-titled *Jagdkommando* 1./128. By the end of that month, the unit had seven Fw 190s available (together with others that were non-serviceable), including three A-5s, an A-6, a G-2 and two G-3s. But on 1 February the *Staffel* was re-designated 10./ZG 1 (some sources dispute this, calling the unit 8./ZG 1). The unit was eventually withdrawn from the Bay of Biscay area of operations and moved to south-central France for purely air-to-ground work. Taking up residence at Lyon-Bron airfield, its Focke-Wulfs were involved in the same type of anti-partisan operations flown by III./SG 4 in the rugged terrain of that part of France. With the *Staffel*'s mixed bag of Fw 190s, 10./ZG 1 was also attached to *Geschwader Bongart*.

Following the Allied landings in the south of France (Operation *Dragoon*) on 15 August 1944, *Geschwader Bongart* was forced to move northwards, joining the general retreat of German forces from the region. Indeed, by early September 1944 it had become obsolete, for with the loss of France, the Germans no longer needed an anti-partisan unit in the West. The *Geschwader* was duly disbanded.

REORGANISATION AND FURTHER COMBAT

In the latter half of 1944, I./SKG 10, the unit that had been such a thorn in the side of Britain's defences on the Channel Front, finally ceased to exist. Since 30 June – on paper at least – it had been known as III./KG 51 and operated under *Stab.*/KG 51 control, but it was apparently not formally renamed as such until 20 October. By then the unit had finally left Normandy for good. Having continued to fight on from Tours until Allied ground forces had forced it to evacuate from northern France, the unit had moved to Mönchen-Gladbach, in western Germany, during September 1944. The *Gruppe* was still commanded by now-Major Kurt Dahlmann.

During that month (on 17 September) the Allies launched Operation *Market Garden* – the ultimately abortive attempt to move deep into the Netherlands by employing airborne assaults to seize key bridges, culminating in the fighting at Arnhem. One of the key objectives for the Luftwaffe in response to *Market Garden* was to destroy the bridges (road and rail) over the River Waal at Nijmegen, which was a key part of the vitally important main route on the way to Arnhem. The area had fallen into Allied hands a short time into the operation, on 20 September, and was being used to hurry troops and armour in the direction of Arnhem. It was therefore vitally important for this crossing to be destroyed as soon as possible, with various Luftwaffe units involved, as well as proposed underwater attacks.

A shadowy Luftwaffe unit, *Sonderstaffel Einhorn* (special [operations] squadron unicorn) was included in the Luftwaffe's response. This *Staffel* appears to have had its roots in a project floated earlier in 1944 concerning proposed suicide attacks by specially trained pilots flying heavily armed Fw 190s against Allied shipping by the secretive KG 200 special operations *Geschwader*. In the event, this plan never materialised, but *Sonderstaffel Einhorn* officially came into being, with its existence (at least on paper)

During the Allied advance into the Netherlands, of which Operation *Market Garden* was a principal part from 17 September 1944, the US Army captured the road and rail bridges over the River Waal at Nijmegen. The Luftwaffe subsequently made repeated attempts to destroy these crossings, with Fw 190 *Jabos* from various units (including *Sonderstaffel Einhorn*) taking part. Both were hit by ordnance dropped by fighter-bombers during this period, and this photograph shows the central span of the railway bridge having clearly been dropped (*Malcolm V Lowe Collection*)

beginning on 5 September 1944 at München-Riem – the new unit also used Vörden at that time. From 20 September the *Staffel* was officially transferred to Achmer, with Holzkirchen also used from the following day.

According to contemporary intelligence decrypts, *Sonderstaffel Einhorn* was subordinated to III./KG 51 for a brief time, but its most famous moments came during the attacks against Nijmegen. The *Staffel*'s Fw 190 *Jabos* were specially adapted so that they could carry a 1000-kg bomb beneath the fuselage, this weapon being amongst the largest ordnance ever dropped from the Focke-Wulf fighter-bomber during its combat career.

On 28 September seven *Sonderstaffel Einhorn* Fw 190s attacked the Nijmegen bridges, and they were credited with hitting each with at least one bomb – the rail bridge suffered significant damage. It is still not clear what type of ordnance these Focke-Wulfs carried, British reports stating that a 500-kg bomb struck the rail bridge, while German accounts from *Luftflotte* 3 headquarters appear to suggest weapons of either 1000- or 1800-kg. The raid was launched from Achmer, the Focke-Wulfs dive-bombing from approximately 5000 ft.

That day was particularly successful for Canadian-manned No 411 Sqn, a Spitfire IX unit of the 2nd Tactical Air Force's No 126 Wing based at B56 Evere, in Belgium. Flg Off M G Graham was one of the squadron's pilots tasked with defending the bridges at Nijmegen on the 28th, and he wrote the following combat report upon returning to base;

'Over Nijmegen 8 plus F.W. 190 were sighted approaching from S.E. at approximately 12–14,000 feet. We climbed into them. I positioned myself approximately 1,500 yards behind one F.W. 190 diving on bridge and closed to approximately 700 yards flying through Allied Flak. F.W. 190 dropped bomb near bridge and did a climbing turn to starboard into cloud. I followed and caught him coming up through top of cloud. Fired from line astern at 500–700 yards. As enemy A/C was flying dead into sun, result of fire was not immediately observed, but enemy aircraft turned port and dived steeply through cloud. I followed and saw A/C fly into ground. F/Lt [J M "Max"] Portz confirmed it as hitting ground and burning. I claim one F.W. 190 Destroyed.'

The Focke-Wulf that Graham shot down was the 'tail-end Charlie' of the dive-bombing attack flown by Leutnant Herbert Leschanz, who was killed when his aircraft crashed.

In early November 1944 *Sonderstaffel Einhorn* was relocated to northern Italy, and later morphed into 13./KG 200 on 1 December 1944, although some contemporary reports suggest that 13./KG 200 was actually formed in January 1945 from 4./KG 200.

As for I./SKG 10 and its transformation into III./KG 51, that nameplate was short-lived. Just 11 days after the official renaming of I./SKG 10 as III./KG 51 on 20 October, it was redesignated *Nachtschlachtgruppe* (NSGr) 20. This new moniker was particularly appropriate due to the unit's normal dusk and nocturnal activities, which had started as far back as the spring of 1943 when I./SKG 10 began night attacks against southern England. The commander of the new unit was none other than Major Kurt Dahlmann, who continued as its leader until war's end. Its initial base was Bonn-Hangelar, where the *Gruppe* had been stationed from 20 September during its time as III./KG 51, having previously used the airfields of Mönchen-Gladbach and Köln-Ostheim for brief periods.

The *Gruppe*'s nocturnal Fw 190 *Jabos* were involved in the ultimately unsuccessful defence of Aachen, which fell on 21 October. This was a significant event, as it was the first important German town to be captured by Allied ground forces. NSGr 20 was subsequently a constituent of *Gefechtsverband Hallensleben,* along with Ju 87-operating NSGrs 1 and 2. Amongst other missions, it flew night operations during the bitter fighting in the Hürtgen Forest area southeast of Aachen.

NSGr 20 was subsequently heavily involved in the major German counter-offensive Operation *Wacht am Rhein* that is often referred to in popular culture as the Ardennes Offensive or the 'Battle of the Bulge'. This began on 16 December 1944, and Fw 190s saw action from the start. Using their night-flying capabilities, several of NSGr 20's pilots acted as pathfinders during the early hours of 17 December to guide paratroop-carrying Ju 52/3m transports for an important drop north of the Belgian town of Malmedy. Virtually throughout the overall Ardennes Offensive, the unit's Fw 190 *Jabos* were involved in nocturnal air-to-ground operations, carrying a variety of ordnance, but often the ubiquitous 250- and 500-kg bombs, in support of Wehrmacht Heer (Army) operations. This was in spite of the often terrible weather conditions during that period.

When St Trond airfield in Belgium was captured by the Allies in September 1944, amongst the damaged and wrecked Luftwaffe aircraft there was Fw 190G-3 Wk-Nr 160699. It is believed to have been operated by I./SKG 10, which at that time was (on paper at least) also known as III./KG 51, a designation that had been delegated to this *Jabo* unit from 30 June 1944 (*EN Archive*)

CHAPTER FIVE

DECLINE AND FALL

Flown by Feldwebel Werner Hohenberg of I./JG 2's *Gruppenstab*, Fw 190D-9 Wk-Nr 210194 was shot down near Stolberg on 1 January 1945 during Operation *Bodenplatte*. Hohenberg was an accomplished fighter pilot, being just the type of capable airman that the Jagdwaffe could ill afford to lose *(Malcolm V Lowe Collection)*

It had been intended that the first day of the major German counter-offensive codenamed *Wacht am Rhein* would also see a significant aerial offensive by the Luftwaffe against Allied forward airfields in Belgium, northeastern France and in the small part of the Netherlands held by Allied ground forces. Eventually named Operation *Bodenplatte*, the plan was for it to be a massive blow against the Allies' aerial dominance and establish air superiority to allow the ground forces to press on with their attack unhindered by US, RAF and Commonwealth aerial assets. This substantial raid was planned to be undertaken by single-engined Luftwaffe fighters acting in the air-to-ground role rather than their established aerial combat activities.

To that end, planning for this ambitious operation had started several weeks earlier, and was intended to include both Fw 190A and Bf 109G/K units acting as temporary *Jabos*. In addition, several of the *Gruppen* involved in *Bodenplatte* were already operating or were in the process of converting onto the Fw 190D-9. This relatively new type had entered service with JG 26 in the late summer/early autumn of 1944. Powered by a Jumo 213 inline engine, the aircraft was definitely not initially designed as a *Jabo*.

It was not intended that the Fw 190s and Bf 109s would carry bombs, the objective instead being for them to use their cannon and machine guns to maximum effect in strafing. Most aircraft would carry a standard

Considerable damage was caused at some Allied airfields that were attacked during Operation *Bodenplatte* on 1 January 1945, with this USAAF P-47D Thunderbolt being destroyed at A92 St Trond. But such losses were easily replaceable. In the case of St Trond, the USAAF fighter-bomber units based there were barely interrupted in their operational flying on 1 January or on any subsequent days as a result of the Jagdwaffe attack (*Malcolm V Lowe Collection*)

300-litre fuel tank beneath the fuselage, this being particularly needed by the Messerschmitts, whose range and endurance were considerably shorter than the longer-legged Focke-Wulfs.

The principal Fw 190 units that took part (with one or more of their *Gruppen* being Focke-Wulf equipped) included JGs 1, 2, 3, 4, 6, 11, 26 and 54, plus SG 4, which had recently returned from the Eastern Front. Except for SG 4, virtually all of these *Geschwader* had been diverted from Reich defence fighter duties in the preceding days of December to help, where possible, the German ground forces when weather permitted, principally with the purpose of trying to clear the skies of Allied aircraft. But they had also continued with their main tasking of trying to combat USAAF daylight high-altitude heavy bomber raids as well. This had spread thinly an already depleted fighter force. By late 1944, the once-proud Jagdwaffe was suffering many casualties, leaving it increasingly reliant on inexperienced pilots recently out of training to fill the gaps left by older, more experienced pilots being lost.

To aid the different *Gruppen* in finding their allotted Allied airfield targets, 'pathfinder' Ju 88Gs, referred to by the Germans as '*Lotsen*', were delegated to lead each unit to the vicinity of the specific airfield that it was to attack. All the German pilots were under orders to avoid contact with any Allied fighters. Writing after *Bodenplatte*, Oberleutnant Emil Clade of Hespe-based III./JG 27, which was a part of the attack force, explained 'We had orders not to interfere in a dogfight'. Indeed, the pilots' instructions in most units included the necessity to maintain strict radio silence until they were returning to base and over friendly territory.

Although the mass attack against Allied airfields had been intended to coincide exactly with the start of the Wehrmacht Heer's ground offensive, bad weather continually interrupted these plans. The winter of 1944–45 in northwest Europe was one of the harshest of the 20th century, and operational flying was totally impossible for several days. These inclement atmospheric conditions grounded both Luftwaffe and Allied air assets. Although a limited number of sorties were flown when the bad weather permitted, the opportunity for the large-scale attack envisaged for *Bodenplatte* was lacking.

It was therefore not launched until 1 January 1945. By then, the German Ardennes offensive had lost momentum on the ground owing to stubborn Allied resistance and clearing weather. The improving weather allowed US, British and Commonwealth aircraft to operate in large numbers against the German ground units, which could no longer count on cover from the Luftwaffe. The Wehrmacht Heer attempted to regain the initiative by launching Operation *Nordwind*, and it was intended that the Luftwaffe would support this new offensive through its *Bodenplatte* mass attack on its now revised time schedule.

The Allies appear to have had little prior specific or detailed knowledge that such a large and coordinated attack was going to take place. Although, therefore, not forewarned, Allied units had nevertheless begun to fill the skies with aircraft going about their 'normal' business of mounting patrols or performing actual attack missions on German tactical targets by around 0900 hrs on 1 January. This meant that the German fighters on their *Bodenplatte* mission were heading towards an enemy that was already alert. Any thoughts that most if not all Allied airmen would be on the ground getting over the New Year's festivities were incorrect.

Many of the attacks carried out on 1 January 1945 during Operation *Bodenplatte* were disorganised, with numerous pilots becoming lost. However, amongst the most successful was the raid led by the high-scoring ace Major Heinz Bär, the *Geschwaderkommodore* of JG 3. The unit's allotted target of B78 Eindhoven airfield in the Netherlands was successfully attacked, with many aircraft destroyed on the ground and Bär himself shooting down two Typhoons (*EN Archive*)

For many of the Luftwaffe fighter pilots who were becoming *Jabo* airmen for the day, it was a sobering experience. The strike force included seasoned pilots, but many of their colleagues were fresh from rudimentary advanced training, with a small number on their first operational sortie.

In its execution, the mass attack proved to be a failure of very serious consequences for the Luftwaffe. The strike force took off from myriad airfields in Germany, with each *Gruppe* allocated a particular Allied air base as its target. Due to the secrecy surrounding the mission, German Flak crews were unaware in advance of the sudden presence of so many Luftwaffe aircraft, and they duly fired on their own pilots, bringing down a number of Focke-Wulfs and Messerschmitts.

Having crossed the frontlines, the German aircraft were at the mercy of Allied light anti-aircraft gun batteries – more were shot down, including some of the pathfinder Ju 88s. Several of the attacking units ran into Allied fighters and more losses ensued. The result was that many *Gruppen* missed their allotted targets, pilots became lost and very few attacks were successfully carried out. Although considerable damage was achieved at several airfields by the impromptu *Jabo* pilots, the Allied losses in terms of aircraft and other equipment were easily replaced in the following weeks.

One of the most successful attacks was carried out by the Focke-Wulfs and Messerschmitts of JG 3, led by the unit's *Kommodore*, Major Heinz Bär. The *Geschwader* reached its allotted target of B78 Eindhoven airfield, in the Netherlands, and attacked for some 25 minutes, causing considerable damage. Bär himself shot down two Typhoons at the start of the attack. He later wrote;

'On New Year's Day a big operation by all *Jagdverbände* over Holland and Belgium. *Jagdgeschwader* 3 attacks Eindhoven: 40–50 aircraft destroyed on the ground and ten in the air – two Tempests [sic] by me at 09.23–09.25. Aerial reconnaissance showed that of the 170 aircraft on the field, 80–100 were destroyed. Bravo!'

But many of the raids by other units were less successful. Amongst them was the intended attack on A92 St Trond, in Belgium, by JG 2 and SG 4, which was a total failure. Instead, the airfield was attacked by a mixed bag of pilots from other *Geschwader* including JG 4. One of this unit's Focke-Wulfs that became erroneously involved at St Trond was Fw 190A-8/R2 Wk-Nr 681497 'White 11' of II.(*Sturm*)/JG 4 flown by Gefreiter Walter Wagner. The aircraft force-landed on, or in the vicinity of, the airfield and Wagner was taken prisoner.

Particularly important losses during the ill-conceived and unsuccessful *Bodenplatte* attack on 1 January were the *Sturm* anti-bomber Focke-Wulfs, which had been temporarily taken off fighter duties and their pilots turned into impromptu *Jabo* airmen. Amongst the Fw 190A-8/R2s lost to the Allies was Wk-Nr 681497 'White 11' of II. (*Sturm*)/JG 4, flown by Gefreiter Walter Wagner in the confused and disjointed attack on St Trond. With the engine of his fighter having been hit, Wagner made a wheels-down landing in the vicinity of the airfield, whereupon he was captured and his former aircraft became the focus of much subsequent activity (*Malcolm V Lowe Collection*)

The Fw 190A-8/R2 of Gefreiter Wagner was repaired by the groundcrew of the 404th FG based at St Trond and made airworthy. Painted in a very high-visibility colour scheme, and escorted by other members of the unit in their Thunderbolts, the group's CO, Lt Col Leo Moon, made at least one flight and possibly several more in the Focke-Wulf (*Malcolm V Lowe Collection*)

As an engineering exercise, groundcrew from the P-47-equipped 404th FG, based at St Trond, made the aircraft airworthy, sourcing a replacement BMW 801 engine from a US depot at Reims, in France. The fighter was painted in an overall bright colour scheme variously described by former members of the unit as red, orange-red or crimson. It bore the black tail 'code' I-I-45 (for 1 January 1945), plus the fuselage 'code' 'OO-L' (the 'L' standing for the 404th FG's CO, Lt Col Leo Moon).

For many years it was believed that the Focke-Wulf was never flown by the 404th. However information in recent years from veteran pilots of the group confirmed that the aircraft was indeed taken aloft on at least one occasion by Lt Col Moon. When the 404th FG subsequently moved from St Trond to another airfield (Y54 Kelz in Germany), the gaudily painted Focke-Wulf was left behind and presumably later scrapped.

Overall, only around a third of the attacking *Gruppen* achieved surprise during *Bodenplatte* and raided their designated target. But far worse for the Luftwaffe, the operation failed to achieve air superiority, even temporarily, leaving the German ground forces exposed to Allied air attack. Even more significantly, a number of experienced pilots were killed or taken prisoner – personnel that the increasingly depleted Luftwaffe could ill afford to lose. *Bodenplatte* was by far the last significant offensive operation mounted by the Luftwaffe during the war.

Independently of *Bodenplatte*, NSGr 20 continued to be an important operator of Fw 190 *Jabos* until war's end, principally undertaking nocturnal missions. Based initially at Bonn-Hangelar until January 1945, it then relocated to Germersheim until March. Showing the nomadic nature of many Luftwaffe units at that time as dictated by the changing war situation, the unit spent several weeks at Twente and Zwolle, in the Netherlands, in March–April, before ending the war at Delmenhorst and Hagenow, in northern Germany. NSGr 20 flew its final sorties of the war on 4 May against British forces west of Lübeck in Schleswig-Holstein.

CHAPTER FIVE DECLINE AND FALL

Following evaluation, some captured Luftwaffe aircraft were flown by No 1426 (Enemy Aircraft) Flight based at RAF Collyweston, in Northamptonshire, to familiarise Allied airmen with the German types they would meet in combat. Photographed in January 1945 framed by Ju 88S-1 Wk-Nr 140604, Fw 190A-5/U8 Wk-Nr 152596, formerly 'White 6' of 1./SKG 10, had been landed in error at RAF Manston during June 1943 and duly became PN999 after being repainted in RAF camouflage (*Malcolm V Lowe Collection*)

But by then any possible effectiveness of the Fw 190 as a *Jabo* in the West had been lost. The aerial battle was all but over before the final unconditional surrender that ended the war in Europe on 8 May 1945. The ever-decreasing number of usable airfields, chronic fuel shortages, the dwindling cadre of experienced pilots and the general war situation finally ended the conflict for the Focke-Wulf *Jabos*.

As a fighter-bomber, the Fw 190 had achieved a great deal in the West since its service introduction in 1942, often to the complete frustration of those on the Allied side who tried to counter the type's operations. Despite Generalmajor Adolf Galland being critical of the diversion of fighter production to meet this specialist task, there were never enough Fw 190 *Jabos* in the right place to really make a difference to the general war situation. No matter how effective the *Jabos* had been during their specific operational deployments, their paucity in number resulted in them having no effect whatsoever on the final outcome of the war.

Hundreds of abandoned Focke-Wulfs were captured by the Allies immediately prior to and at the end of World War 2. One of the many was this wrecked Fw 190F-8 at Rhein-Main, the aircraft having formerly been assigned to 11./KG 200 – it bears the *Geschwader*'s 'A3' code. This *Staffel*, alongside NSGr 20, flew bombing sorties against the newly captured Remagen bridge over the Rhine in early March 1945 (*EN Archive*)

APPENDICES

COLOUR PLATES COMMENTARY

1
Fw 190A-2 Wk-Nr 299 'Blue 2' + 'Chevron and Bar' of 10.(*Jabo*)/JG 2, Caen-Carpiquet, France, August 1942
This aircraft is finished in a standard mid-war grey camouflage scheme of RLM 74/75 splinter pattern on its uppersurfaces, with RLM 76 blue-grey on the undersurfaces and fuselage sides. Wk-Nr 299 was a very early Focke-Wulf *Jabo* (which has also been described in the past as an A-3) with comparatively light mottling on its fuselage. With a yellow rudder and nose underside, it bore the famous unit emblem of 10.(*Jabo*)/JG 2 (a dark red/brown fox with a broken ship in its mouth) and the blue 'chevron and bar' associated with fighter-bomber *Staffeln* on the rear fuselage, as previously worn by the unit's Bf 190F *Jabos*.

2
Fw 190A-2 Wk-Nr 122080 'Black 13' + 'Chevron and Bomb' of Oberfeldwebel Werner Kassa, 10.(*Jabo*)/JG 26, Saint-Omer-Wizernes, France, August 1942
Painted in standard camouflage, Wk-Nr 122080 was again a very early Focke-Wulf *Jabo* with comparatively light mottling. This aircraft features the stylised motif (a modified bomb from the 'chevron and bar' marking used by *Jabo*-operating *Staffeln* on the Channel Front) on the rear fuselage. Unique to the unit's Fw 190 *Jabos*, it was different to the bomb symbol worn by the *Staffel*'s Bf 109F *Jabos* that the Focke-Wulfs replaced. The Fw 190A-2 also features a yellow rudder and nose underside. On 26 August 1942, Oberfeldwebel Kassa was one of two pilots who raided Eastbourne, and he was shot down and killed in this aircraft by Pvt E G Johnstone of the Canadian Seaforth Highlanders.

3
Fw 190A-2 or A-3 Wk-Nr 080 'Blue 6' + 'Chevron and Bar' of 10.(*Jabo*)/JG 2, Caen-Carpiquet, France, summer 1942
Again in standard camouflage, Wk-Nr 080 also has comparatively light mottling and a yellow rudder and nose underside. The unit badge, consisting of a dark red/brown fox with a broken ship in its mouth, was almost certainly painted on the aircraft's cowling. Although most likely an Fw 190A-2, Wk-Nr 080 is sometimes referred to as an A-3.

4
Fw 190A-4/U8 'Blue 11' + 'Chevron and Bar' of 10.(*Jabo*)/JG 2, Istres-le Tubé, southern France, late November 1942
Finished in standard camouflage, this aircraft features heavy mottling that was probably unit-applied. With the standard yellow rudder and nose underside, this unidentified Fw 190A-4/U8 is marked with the unusual blue 'Chevron and Bar' marking unique to 10.(*Jabo*)/JG 2 on the rear fuselage – the symbol combination was a carryover from the *Staffel*'s time with the Bf 109F-4/B. This aircraft was part of the brief, and uneventful, deployment made by the two Channel Front *Jabo* units to Istres-le Tubé following the Allies' Operation *Torch* landings on the North African coast.

5
Fw 190A-3 Wk-Nr 467 'Blue 12' + 'Chevron and Bar' of Leutnant Leopold 'Poldi' Wenger, 10.(*Jabo*)/JG 2, Caen-Carpiquet, France, early 1943
Camouflaged in the standard scheme, this aircraft also has comparatively light mottling and a yellow rudder and nose underside. Leutnant Wenger flew the aircraft on several significant *Jabo* raids, including the attack against Teignmouth on 10 January 1943 that resulted in Wk-Nr 467 suffering battle damage.

6
Fw 190A-5/U8 Wk-Nr 150532 'Black 4' + 'Chevron and Bomb' of 10.(*Jabo*)/JG 26, Saint-Omer-Wizernes, France, circa January 1943
Featuring standard camouflage, Wk-Nr 150532 also has comparatively light mottling and a yellow rudder and nose underside. It is also marked with the stylised bomb marking unique to the Fw 190 fighter-bombers of 10.(*Jabo*)/JG 26 on its rear fuselage. The aircraft is armed with a single 500-kg weapon on its ETC 501 underfuselage stores pylon.

7
Fw 190A-4/U8 Wk-Nr 142409 'Black 2' + 'Chevron and Bomb' of Leutnant Hermann Hoch, 10.(*Jabo*)/JG 26, Abbeville-Drucat, France, 20 January 1943
With standard camouflage, this aircraft features heavy mottling that was probably unit-applied, as well as the ubiquitous yellow rudder and nose underside. Leutnant Hoch was part of the strike force on the notorious 20 January 1943 raid against London during which Sandhurst School in Catford was bombed, killing 38 children and five teachers. Having crash-landed Wk-Nr 142409 near Capel after being hit by anti-aircraft fire, Hoch destroyed the fighter-bomber with an explosive charge before being taken prisoner.

8
Fw 190A-5/U8 'Black Triangle' + 'White 1' of II./SKG 10, Caen-Carpiquet, France, March 1943
This relatively new Focke-Wulf *Jabo* features standard camouflage, no mottling whatsoever and the yellow rudder and nose underside synonymous with this period. The aircraft bears the white-outlined black *Schlacht* triangle, which was inappropriate for *Jabo* Focke-Wulfs – several deliveries to SKG 10 featured aircraft painted at the factory in this way.

9
Fw 190A-4/U8 Wk-Nr 147155 'Yellow H' of Feldwebel Otto Bechtold, 7./SKG 10, Amiens-Glisy, April 1943
Part of this aircraft's standard camouflage has been temporarily painted black for nocturnal operations. Black has also been used to tone down/obscure the national markings and the fighter-bomber's 'Yellow H' aircraft identifier. The black 'paint' appears to have been a thick paste-like material variously described after the aircraft's capture (at RAF West Malling on 16–17 April 1943) as 'lamp black' or an 'oil-lamp black mixture'.

10
Fw 190A-4/U8 Wk-Nr 147155 'Yellow H' of Feldwebel Otto Bechtold, 7./SKG 10, RAF West Malling, Kent, 17 April 1943

Wk-Nr 147155 changed sides on the night of 16–17 April 1943 following its unexpected arrival at RAF West Malling. In order to keep prying eyes away the aircraft, and the cockpit in particular (thus avoiding any of its instruments being 'souvenired'), the fighter-bomber had warnings chalked or scratched onto its thick black-finished fuselage side. It appears that no photographs exist of the Focke-Wulf's port side, confirming whether such warnings were repeated there too.

11
Fw 190A-5/U8 'Blue 12' + 'Chevron and Bar' of Leutnant Leopold Wenger, Caen-Carpiquet, 10.(*Jabo*)/JG 2, early spring 1943

In standard camouflage, this aircraft features heavy mottling that was probably unit-applied – this has also extended to the yellow panel beneath the nose, although the rudder has not been touched. Note the small '12' in blue on the engine cowling – an unusual repetition of the aircraft's identifying number.

12
Fw 190A-5/U8 'White A' of 13./SKG 10, Caen-Carpiquet, May 1943

Painted in standard camouflage, 'White A', like 'White E' in profile 3, has a very heavily unit-applied mottle that has seen its fuselage cross and other markings partly oversprayed to make them less conspicuous. Its yellow rudder is untouched, however, although the nose underside panel is now black.

13
Fw 190A-5/U8 'White E' of Leutnant Leopold Wenger, Caen-Carpiquet, 13./SKG 10, 23 May 1943

Also the topic of profile 11, this aircraft is seen in the colours and marking applied following 10.(*Jabo*)/JG 2's redesignation as 13./SKG 10 in April 1943. Again, heavy mottling is clearly in evidence, as is the unmarked yellow rudder and black underside nose panel. Re-coded 'White E', the aircraft's 'Blue 12' + 'Chevron and Bar' on the fuselage have been overpainted and IV. *Gruppe*'s black squiggle applied. Inexplicably, the Fw 190A-5/U8 retains a small '12', now in white, on the engine cowling. As with 'White A', the fighter-bomber's fuselage cross and other markings have been partly oversprayed to make them less conspicuous.

14
Fw 190A-4/U8 Wk-Nr 145843 'Red 9' of Unteroffizier Heinz Ehrhardt, 2./SKG 10, Caen-Carpiquet, France, May 1943

Although some of 'Red 9's' standard camouflage can be seen, much of its RLM 76 blue-grey undersurfaces have been temporarily painted black. The same shade has also been used to tone down/obscure the national markings, but not the aircraft's 'Red 9' identifying number. The fighter-bomber also has a quarter of its spinner painted white. On the night of 20 May 1943, Unteroffizier Ehrhardt became lost during a *Jabo* sortie and landed this aircraft in error at RAF Manston. Wk-Nr 145843 was later allocated the serial number PM679 and assigned to RAE Farnborough and then the Air Fighting Development Unit.

It was damaged in June 1944 and subsequently used as a spares source for No 1426 (Enemy Aircraft) Flight's Fw 190A-5/U8 PN999 (formerly Wk-Nr 152596).

15
Fw 190A-5/U8 Wk-Nr 151353 'Black Chevron and Disc' of *Gruppenadjutant* Oberleutnant Kurt Hevler, *Stab* IV./SKG 10, Caen-Carpiquet, France, 4 June 1943

This aircraft's standard camouflage and yellow rudder and underside nose panel were heavily mottled almost certainly at unit level. On 4 June 1943, Oberleutnant Hevler was part of an 18-strong *Jabo* raid on Eastbourne. When his aircraft was hit by anti-aircraft fire, he attempted to make a forced landing on marshland behind the Star Inn at Normans Bay but the fighter-bomber overturned upon hitting soft ground and Hevler was killed in the subsequent crash.

16
Fw 190A-5/U8 Wk-Nr 152596 'White 6' of Unteroffizier Werner Öhne, 1./SKG 10, Poix, France, June 1943

Another Fw 190 *Jabo* with its standard camouflage and markings temporarily obscured with black paint, this aircraft still has its identifying number, 'White 6', clearly visible and parts of its yellow rudder can also be seen. Although not depicted here, a quarter of its spinner was white. On the night of 20 June 1943, Unteroffizier Öhne became lost during a *Jabo* sortie against Ramsgate and landed in error at RAF Manston. The aircraft was later allocated the serial number PN999 and flew for a time with the RAF's No 1426 (Enemy Aircraft) Flight.

17
Fw 190G-3 'White 9' of 1./SKG 10, Normandy, France, June 1944

Seen in standard camouflage, with heavy mottling that was probably unit-applied, this aircraft (complete with Focke-Wulf drop tank carriers beneath both wings) was one of SKG 10's prized Fw 190Gs. It was photographed hidden under tree cover to avoid being spotted by the many Allied aircraft in the air over Normandy during the D-Day period.

18
Fw 190F-8 'Brown 0' + 'Brown I' of 9./SG 4, Avord, France, summer 1944

Again in standard camouflage with heavy mottling (but with the latter not obscuring its markings), this aircraft is from III./SG 4. Its Fw 190s are amongst the least-known of the France-based Focke-Wulfs that were thrown into action against the Allied invasion forces during and after 6 June 1944. This colour scheme is a reconstruction based on limited available sources.

19
Fw 190A-4/U8 PE882 (formerly Wk-Nr 147155 'Yellow H') of No 1426 (Enemy Aircraft) Flight, RAF Collyweston, Northamptonshire, October 1944

Following its landing in error at RAF West Malling on 16–17 April 1943, Wk-Nr 147155 'Yellow H' was repainted in RAF colours and allocated the serial number PE882. It was camouflaged in Dark Green/Dark Earth uppersurfaces with Yellow undersides, and the Focke-Wulf's ETC 501 bomb/drop tank pylon was partly removed, as depicted here. Although an RAF serial and roundels were applied, the 'last three' of its Wk-Nr were retained on its fin. The aircraft was destroyed in a fatal crash on 13 October 1944, by which time it is believed to have had its Dark Earth areas overpainted in Ocean Grey, as seen in this profile.

20
Fw 190D-9 Wk-Nr 210194 'Black Chevron and Bars' of Feldwebel Werner Hohenberg, *Stab* I./JG 2, Merzhausen, Germany, 1 January 1945
Depicted in late war camouflage of RLM 75 grey and a green (probably RLM 83) on its uppersurfaces and RLM 76 on the fuselage sides, undersurfaces and fin/rudder, this aircraft also features a white spiral on its black spinner and a distinctive yellow/white/yellow JG 2 *Reichsverteidigung* rear fuselage band. One of the valuable Fw 190D-9 fighters delegated to Operation *Bodenplatte* that was lost on 1 January 1945, it was amongst the scattered attackers of St Trond airfield. Wk-Nr 210194 was shot down by a US Army anti-aircraft battery whilst Feldwebel Werner Hohenberg was attempting to head home – he became a PoW.

21
Fw 190A-8/R2 Wk-Nr 681497 'White 11' of Gefreiter Walter Wagner, II.(*Sturm*)/JG 4, Darmstadt-Griesheim, Germany, 1 January 1945
Aside from its weathered camouflage, Wk-Nr 681497 also has a black/white/black *Reichsverteidigung* rear fuselage band synonymous with JG 4. The knight's helmet insignia of 4. *Staffel* was applied exclusively to the left side of the cowling. This aircraft was one of many 'normal' fighters that were taken off Reich defence duty for participation in Operation *Bodenplatte*. JG 4 was supposed to attack A89 Le Culot and Y32 Ophoven, but its pilots became lost, with some attacking St Trond instead. 'White 11' force-landed on, or in the vicinity of, the latter airfield and Gefreiter Walter Wagner was taken prisoner.

22
Fw 190A-8/R2 I-I-45 OO-L (formerly Wk-Nr 681497 'White 11') of the 404th FG, A92 St Trond, Belgium, early 1945
Following its force landing, Gefreiter Wagner's Fw 190A-8/R2 was repaired by groundcrew from the 404th FG at St Trond and returned to airworthiness. The aircraft was painted in an overall bright colour scheme variously described by former unit members as red, orange-red or crimson, with standard late-war US national insignia applied. It also featured the tail 'code' I-I-45 (for 1 January 1945) and the fuselage 'code' 'OO-L' (the 'L' standing for the 404th FG's CO, Lt Col Leo Moon). Although it was believed that the Focke-Wulf was never flown by the 404th, information in recent years from veteran pilots of the group confirmed that the fighter was indeed taken aloft on at least one occasion by Lt Col Moon.

SELECTED SOURCES

Bekker, Cajus, *The Luftwaffe War Diaries – The German Air Force in World War II*, Ballantine Books, 1975

Beleznay, Angela, *Incident 48 – Raid on a South Coast Town 1943*, Natula Publications, 2012

Forsyth, Robert, et. al., *Schlachtflieger – Luftwaffe Ground-attack Units 1937–1945*, Midland Publishing, 2007

Galland, Adolf, *The First and the Last*, Methuen, 1955

Goss, Chris, with Cornwell, Peter, and Rauchbach, Bernd, *Luftwaffe Fighter-Bombers over Britain – The Tip and Run Campaign 1942–1943*, Crécy Publishing, 2013

Laureau, Patrick, *Condor – The Luftwaffe in Spain 1936–1939*, Hikoki Publications, 2000

Lowe, Malcolm V, *Osprey Combat Aircraft 149 – Bf 109 Jabo Units in the West*, Osprey Publishing, 2023

Lowe, Malcolm V, *Osprey Production Line To Frontline 5 – Focke Wulf Fw 190*, Osprey Publishing, 2003

Manhro, John, and Pütz, Ron, *Bodenplatte: The Luftwaffe's Last Hope – The Attack on Allied Airfields New Year's Day 1945*, Hikoki Publications, 2004

Mombeek, Eric, *Luftwaffe Colours Volume One Section 2 – Jagdwaffe: The Spanish Civil War*, Classic Publications, 1999

Olynyk, Frank, *Stars and Bars – A Tribute to the American Fighter Ace 1920–1973*, Grub Street, 1995

Parker, Nigel, *Luftwaffe Crash Archive (various volumes)*, Red Kite, 2013–16

Price, Alfred, *Luftwaffe Handbook 1939–1945*, Ian Allan, 1977

Shores, Christopher, and Thomas, Chris, *2nd Tactical Air Force Volume Two – Breakout to Bodenplatte July 1944 to January 1945*, Classic Publications, 2005

Stedman, Robert, *Osprey Warrior 122 – Jagdflieger: Luftwaffe Fighter Pilot 1939–45*, Osprey Publishing, 2008

Ullmann, Michael, *Luftwaffe Colours 1935–1945*, Hikoki Publications, 2002

Weal, John, *Osprey Aircraft of the Aces 68 – Bf 109 Defence of the Reich Aces*, Osprey Publishing, 2006

Weal, John, *Osprey Aviation Elite Units 1 – Jagdgeschwader 2 'Richthofen'*, Osprey Publishing, 2000

Weal, John, *Osprey Aviation Elite Units 12 – Jagdgeschwader 27 'Afrika'*, Osprey Publishing, 2003

Weal, John, *Osprey Aviation Elite Units 13 – Luftwaffe Schlachtgruppen*, Osprey Publishing, 2003

Weal, John, *Osprey Aviation Elite Units 22 – Jagdgeschwader 51 'Mölders'*, Osprey Publishing, 2006

Weal, John, *Osprey Aviation Elite Units 25 – Jagdgeschwader 53 'Pik As'*, Osprey Publishing, 2007

Albert F Simpson Historical Research Center, *USAF Credits for the Destruction of Enemy Aircraft, World War II: USAF Historical Study No. 85*, USAF Air University, Maxwell Air Force Base, Alabama, 1978

Transcripts and notes from interviews with former Luftwaffe personnel, including interview text from the John Batchelor archive

INDEX

Note: numbers in **bold** refer to illustrations.

aircraft
  Bf 109: 14–15, 16–19
  F-6C 79
  Spitfire 19, 26–27, 50–51, 59–60
  Thunderbolt 77, **88**
  Typhoon 28
  see also Fw 190
Ardennes Offensive (1944–45) 86, 89
armament
  bombs **8**, **12**, **13**, **29**, **31**, **83**
  Fw 190: 7, 8, 9–10, **10**, 12–13
  Spitfire 60
  Typhoon 28
  underwing fitments **7**, 8, **10**
  W.Gr.21 rockets **2–3**, 71–74, **73**
Ashford 51

Ball, Flg Off Geoffrey 30–31
Bär, Major Heinz **89**, 90
Bechtold, Feldwebel Otto cp.**9–10** (41, 93), 55, 56
Bell, Flg Off Clive 48
Berkeley, HMS **24**, 25
Blackwell, Plt Off Sam 34
Blase, Feldwebel Karl 22–23, 24, 48
Bodmin **22**, 23
Bognor Regis 27
Bournemouth 25, 57–59, **57**, **58**
Brighton 51–52, 59
Britain, Battle of (1940–41) 14–17, 35
Broadstairs 61–62
Busch, Leutnant Erwin 51–52, 53

Canterbury 29–30
Caulfield, 1Lt Peter 78–79

D-Day (1944) 65–74, 76–82
Dahlmann, Hauptmann Kurt 66, **66**, 82–83, 84, 86
Dartmouth 19–20
Davidson, Flg Off George 21
drop tanks **7**, 8, 12, **12**, **55**, **65**, **69**

Eastbourne 25–26, 35, 48, 50, 52, 62–63, **63**
Ebersparcher, Hauptmann Helmut 66–67
Ehrhardt, Unteroffizier Heinz cp.**14** (43, 94), 56–57
engines 17, 10, 19, **61**, 87
Exmouth 49

Felixstowe 62
Fischer, Leutnant Wolfgang 71–74, **72**
Folkestone 33, 52, 60
Fw 190
  190A 'Black 6' **14**
  190A-1: **6**, 7, 19
  190A-2: 7
  190A-2 Wk-Nr 299 'Blue 2' + 'Chevron and Bar' cp.**1** (37, 93)
  190A-2 Wk-Nr 122080 'Black 13' + 'Chevron and Bomb' 25–26, **25**, cp.**2** (37, 93)
  190A-2 Wk-Nr 122081 'Blue 3' **31**
  190A-2 or A-3 Wk-Nr 080 'Blue 6' + 'Chevron and Bar' **21**, cp.**3** (38, 93)
  190A-3: 7–8
  190A-3 Wk-Nr 467 'Blue 12' + 'Chevron and Bar' **23**, 34, cp.**5** (39, 93)
  190A-3 Wk-Nr 130420 'Black 7' **27**, 28
  190A-4: **2–3**, 8
  190A-4/U8: 8, 11, **29**
  190A-4/U8 'Blue 11' + 'Chevron and Bar' cp.**4** (38, 93)
  190A-4/U8 PE882 (formerly Wk-Nr 147155 'Yellow H') cp.**19** (46, 94)
  190A-4/U8 Wk-Nr 142409 'Black 2' + 'Chevron and Bomb' 30, **33**, 36, cp.**7** (40, 93)
  190A-4/U8 Wk-Nr 145843 'Red 9' cp.**14** (43, 94)
  190A-4/U8 Wk-Nr 147155 'Yellow H' cp.**9–10** (41, 93–94), **55**, 56, **56**
  190A-5: 8–9
  190A-5/U2: **11**
  190A-5/U8: **12**
  190A-5/U8 'Black Triangle' + 'White 1' cp.**8** (40, 93)
  190A-5/U8 'Blue 12' + 'Chevron and Bar' cp.**11** (42, 94), **59**
  190A-5/U8 'White A' cp.**12** (42, 94)
  190A-5/U8 'White E' cp.**13** (43, 94)
  190A-5/U8 Wk-Nr 150532 'Black 4' + 'Chevron and Bomb' cp.**6** (39, 93)
  190A-5/U8 Wk-Nr 151353 'Black Chevron and Disc' cp.**15** (44, 94)
  190A-5/U8 Wk-Nr 152596 'White 6' cp.**16** (44, 94), 64, **92**
  190A-6: 9, **73**
  190A-7L 9
  190A-8: 9–10
  190A-8/R2: **80**
  190A-8/R2 I-I-45 OO-L (formerly Wk-Nr 681497 'White 11') cp.**22** (47, 95), 91
  190A-8/R2 Wk-Nr 681497 'White 11' cp.**21** (47, 95), 90–91, **90**, **91**
  190D-9: 87
  190D-9 Wk-Nr 210194 'Black Chevron and Bars' cp.**20** (46, 95), 87
  190F 11–12
  190F-8: **92**
  190F-8 'Brown O' + 'Brown I' cp.**18** (45, 94)
  190G 11, 12–13
  190G-3: **7**, **8**, 13
  190G-3 'White 9' cp.**17** (45, 94), **69**
  190G-3 Wk Nr 160699: **86**
  190G-8: 13

Graham, Flg Off M G 85
Gray, Lt Col Frederic C Jr 77–78
Great Yarmouth 54

Haabjørn, Flt Lt Erik 52–53
Harries, Sqn Ldr Raymond 60
Hastings 27, 28, 50, 57
Hesse, Oberleutnant Heinrich 79, 80
Hevler, Oberleutnant Kurt cp.**15** (44, 94), 62, 63
Hoch, Leutnant Hermann 33, 36, cp.**7** (40, 93)
Höfer, Unteroffizier Walter 24, 26
Hohenberg, Feldwebel Werner cp.**20** (46, 95), 87

Immervoll, Unteroffizier Alfred 48, **48**
Ipswich 62
Isle of Wight 19, 33, 35, 52, 61
Italy 75

Kassa, Oberfeldwebel Werner 25–26
Keller, Leutnant Paul 20, 32, 51

Lallemant, Flg Off Raymond 32, 36
Laue, Gefreiter Karl **58**, 60, **62**
Laval 76, 79, 80, 81, 82
Liesendahl, Hauptmann Frank 16–18, **17**, 20
London **33**, 35–48, 50–51
Lorient 53–54
Lowestoft 54–55
Luftwaffe units
  ErprGr 210: 14–15, 16
  Geschwader Bongart 83, 84
  JG 1: 88
  JG 2: 16–20, **21**, **22**, 22–27, 29–31, **31**, 33–52, cp.**1** (37, 93), cp.**3–5** (38–39, 93), cp.**11** (62, 94), cp.**20** (46, 95), 71–74, 88
  JG 3: **80**, 88, **89**
  JG 4: cp.**21** (47, 95), 88, 90, **90**
  JG 6: 88
  JG 11: 82, 88

JG 26: **14**, 16, 18, 20–21, 23–33, **25**, **29**, 35–51, cp.**2** (37, 93), cp.**6–7** (39–40, 93), 62, 67–69, 74–75, 88
JG 54: 49–53
KG 200: 13, 85, **92**
LG 2: 15
NSGr 20: 86, 91
SAGr 128: 83–84
SG 4: cp.**18** (45, 94), 75–77, 79, 81, 88, 90
SKG 10: **7**, cp.**8–10** (40–41, 93–94), cp.**12–17** (42–45, 94), 50–57, **55**, **57**, 59–67, **59**, **60**, **62**, **65**, **66**, 69–71, **69**, **70**, **71**, 75, 82–84, **83**, 86
Sonderstaffel Einhorn 84–85
ZG 1: 83, 84
ZG 2: 29–31

Margate 61–62
Maximowitz, Unteroffizier Willi **80**
McElhare, 1Lt William 77
Müller, Oberleutnant Kurt 31, 32

Needham, Flg Off Barry 27
Nippa, Leutnant Erhard 24, 53

Öhne, Unteroffizier Werner cp.**16** (44, 94), 64
Operation
  Bodenplatte (1945) 87–91, **87**, **88**
  Jubilee (1942) 23–25, **24**
  Market Garden (1944) 84–85, **85**
  Steinbock (1944) 64
Osterkamp, Generalmajor Theodor 15, 18

passengers **76**
Plunser, Hauptmann Karl 18, 20
Powell, Plt Off Lloyd 27
Priller, Oberleutnant Josef 'Pips' 67–69, **68**

radar 35, 55
Ramsgate **27**, 28
Rennes (submarine chaser) 19–20, **20**
Robb, Plt Off Ken 21

Saint-Aubin-sur-Mer 79–80
Salcombe 51, 52
Salisbury 23
Sames, Sgt Artie 28–29
Schmidt, Unteroffizier Friedrich-Karl 57–58, **57**, **58**
Schröter, Major Fritz 20, 24–25, 75
Schumann, Leutnant Heinz 21, 53
Setzer, Leutnant Fritz 50, 56
Streich, Unteroffizier Eugen **58**, 59, **60**

tactics 17
Teignmouth 30, 34
Thomas, Plt Off Gordon 28–29
Thompson, Sgt Richard 49
Torbay/Torquay 26–27, **26**, 29, 33, 60–61, **61**, **62**
Townsend, Flg Off John 54
training 32

Wagner, Gefreiter Walter cp.**21–22** (47, 95), 90, 91
Wenger, Leutnant Leopold 19–20, **23**, 24–25, 27, 34, 53, **59**, 62–63
  mounts cp.**5** (39, 93), cp.**11** (42, 94), cp.**13** (43, 94)
Weyert, Major Gerhard 75, 76, 81–82, 83
Wodarczyk, Unteroffizier Heinz **68**, 69

Yeovil 22–23

Zebrowski, Oberfähnrich Wolfgang 66, 69–71